A Love Story

MILDRED MARSHALL'S STORY
as written by ROBERT MARSHALL

LUCIDBOOKS

I've Got This: A Love Story

Copyright © 2025 by Robert Marshall

Published by Lucid Books in Houston, TX
www.LucidBooks.com

All rights reserved. No part of this publication may be reproduced, stored in a retrieval system, or transmitted in any form by any means, electronic, mechanical, photocopy, recording, or otherwise, without the prior permission of the publisher, except as provided for by USA copyright law.

Unless otherwise indicated, scripture quotations are taken from the (NIV) Holy Bible, New International Version®, NIV®. Copyright ©1973, 1978, 1984, 2011 by Biblica, Inc.™ Used by permission of Zondervan. All rights reserved worldwide. www.zondervan.com The "NIV" and "New International Version" are trademarks registered in the United States Patent and Trademark Office by Biblica, Inc.™

ISBN: 978-1-63296-768-8 (Paperback)
ISBN: 978-1-63296-769-5 (Hardback)
eISBN: 978-1-63296-770-1

Special Sales: Most Lucid Books titles are available in special quantity discounts. Custom imprinting or excerpting can also be done to fit special needs. Contact Lucid Books at Info@LucidBooks.com

To Mildred, My Special Angel

CONTENTS

Special Thanks vii
Foreword ix
The Early Years 3
The Abuse Years 4
The Virginia Years 8
God's Plan 11
The Yuppie Years 14
The True Love Years 18
The Beginning of a New Life 24
Post-Cancer (PC) Days
    Day 1 – Facing New Days (Mildred) 28
    Days 2 through 2,040 – (Bob) 30
Epilogue 289

SPECIAL THANKS

Mildred and I wish to thank Marie Jones (Mildred's sister), Mary Lashendock (my sister), Robert Lashendock for his photography work, and countless friends and New Life Church members, all of whom walked the entire cancer journey with us. During the five-and-a-half years of our journey, they were with us, no matter how difficult the journey was. We will be forever grateful.

FOREWORD

Written by Bob Marshall

This book is the life and faith story of Mildred Marshall. She truly was one of God's special angels sent to this earth to minister to everyone she came in contact with. She had the most rock-solid, unshakable, doubt-free faith of any person I have ever known. She also had the most God-like ability to forgive and extend grace to anyone who ever hurt her. I was blessed to have her as part of my life every day for almost 40 years. I certainly did not deserve someone as special as she was, but I think our Heavenly Father determined that I needed all the help I could get, and she was the person up to the job. She transformed me into the person I am today. I will love her always and forever.

Mildred's entire life reflected her favorite words of the Bible

The Lord is my shepherd, I lack nothing. He makes me lie down in green pastures, he leads me beside quiet waters, he refreshes my soul. He guides me along the right paths for his name's sake. Even though I walk through the darkest valley, I will fear no evil, for you are with me; your rod and your staff, they comfort me. You prepare a table before me in the presence of my enemies. You anoint my head with oil; my cup overflows. Surely your goodness and love will follow me all the days of my life, and I will dwell in the house of the Lord forever.

—Ps. 23 (NIV)

Our hope is that Mildred's story will impart God's love to all who read it, that it will inspire all who are walking through their own personal valleys to cry out to our God so He can say to you what He said to Mildred and me.

"I'VE GOT THIS."

"I'VE GOT THIS."

The following seven chapters and Day 1 of the CaringBridge journal were spoken by Mildred Marshall and written by Bob Marshall

The Early Years

I was born at home on August 28, 1948, in Robeson County, North Carolina, a county notorious for having one of the highest violent crime rates in the state. My birth certificate wasn't issued until my Aunt Edna filed for a Delayed Certificate of Birth on September 19, 1961. My parents were Lumbee Indian illiterate sharecroppers who farmed the land with crops such as tobacco, corn, cotton, and cucumbers. It was very hard work. I had four younger brothers, two younger sisters, one older half-brother, and one older half-sister.

All the children worked the farm from the young age of eight. When we went into the fields to work the tobacco in the early mornings, the leaves were so wet from the dew that we became very cold and numb. When we worked the cotton, our fingers became very sore and frequently bled. I saw how my mother got up at 4:00 a.m., fixed breakfast, went out in the fields until 10:30 a.m., returned to the house to fix lunch, went back to the fields, and then returned to the house at 4:00 p.m. to make dinner. The children helped my mother clean the kitchen, and then she helped them with their baths. I learned at a very early age that this was not something

I wanted to do. I think you can understand why I don't know how my Mom did it, but for saving grace.

The Abuse Years

I did not have a good father. He was a violent alcoholic who was physically abusive to my mom, as well as the children. By the time I was 10 years old, my older half-brother and older half-sister had left home because they could not take the abuse any longer. I did not know where they went or what happened to them. My mother left North Carolina in August 1959. She left in order to save her own life. Her husband told her she could not take any of us with her, and none of us knew where she went. We remained in that house for some time after she left. I had to learn to take care of my brothers and sisters—cook for them, clean up after them, and get them bathed and off to school. That is when everything started.

My father would leave us for days while he went off drinking with his brothers. Then he would come home and violently beat us. I remember all of us crawling underneath the beds so he could not reach us. When he was drunk, he was evil. He would come home and have his way with me. What he did was not sex. It was pure unleashed anger and rage. If I did anything to resist, he would beat me even more and threaten to do the same to my two younger sisters. Soon after, he moved all of us into his mother's house. My father's two brothers, his sister, and her two children also lived there. Even while we were living there, the abuse continued.

Finally, my cousin Mar Ree came by to talk with me one day, and she stayed overnight. She had figured out what my father was doing to me. She asked me about it, and at first, I could not tell her what was happening. When my father found out we had talked, he beat me so badly that I literally could not stand up straight for two weeks. Another night when Mar Ree was there, my father came home and insisted I get in bed with him. When I said no, he attacked me and forced me into bed. Mar Ree was in one of the other bedrooms. The next morning she asked me what happened, and I did not know what to say to her.

It was during this time that my grandmother had a stroke. She, too, had determined what was happening. She told me I should run away, but I was only 11 years old at the time. I could not leave my sisters and brothers. Besides, where would I go? We lived in the country. I did not realize there were people who could help me.

That is when my Heavenly Father took over in the form of my Aunt Edna, my mother's sister. Mar Ree had told her what was happening. She immediately came to see all of us and brought clothes and food. We were all so happy to see her. She asked me what my father was doing to me, and at first, I could not tell her. I did not know how to explain it to her. After she left, my father was gone for several days. We later found out he had been arrested and put in jail. We were all so happy that he could not beat us while he was locked up. But he was soon released, and then he came home. He was angrier than ever and threatened to beat me to death if I did not do what he wanted me to do.

Once again, Aunt Edna came to see us. She asked me again what my father was doing to me. This time, I was able to tell her. She immediately left and returned with the police. They confronted my father, who denied everything. At that point, I had to confront him while the police and my aunt were standing there. He still denied that anything had happened, but the police did not believe him. They immediately arrested him and put him back in jail. He was later tried, convicted, and sentenced to five to 10 years in prison.

I am so thankful my father never sexually abused my two younger sisters, Marie and Carrie. After my father went to prison, Aunt Edna brought all seven of us to her house to live with her. Also living there were her four children and our older half-sister, Sylvia, who unbeknownst to us had been living with Aunt Edna. Finally, I was able to sleep in peace without worrying what might happen that night or the next day. Finally, I was able to live each day without fear and absolute terror. After we began living with Aunt Edna, she took me to a doctor to be examined. The doctor who performed the examination said it was the absolute worst case of sexual abuse he had ever seen.

After some time passed, Aunt Edna told me I had to go with her. I wanted to know where we were going. She brought me to the prison and made me face my father who was behind bars. I was crying and did not want to do that, but she told me I would understand one day. I was hurt that she would make me do it. I did not understand at the time that she was teaching me how to forgive.

Aunt Edna knew where my mother was staying and contacted her. In April 1961, my mother came back and took my two youngest brothers to Portsmouth, Virginia, to live with her. Then in December 1962, when I was 14 years old, my mother returned to North Carolina to take the rest of us back with her to Virginia. Sylvia wanted to remain in North Carolina to finish her senior year of high school, and then she joined the Army. The rest of us continued to live in Portsmouth with our mother and stepfather, John Caldwell. In 1963, my older half-brother moved to Virginia, and for the first time since 1959, all nine of us children were reunited. Oh what a joyous day it was!

When I was 18, I recalled the day my aunt took me to the prison and taught me about forgiveness. I had a lot of anger in my heart and soul because of what my father had done to me. I did not like men at all. However, on that day at the prison, I finally understood and gave it all to my Heavenly Father. All of a sudden, all that anger, frustration, and bitterness were gone. My aunt knew I had to face my demons, and only by doing so and releasing all the pain to God would I be free of it.

I loved my Aunt Edna so much. If it had not been for her, I do not know what would have happened to all of us. We probably would have been placed in various foster homes by the Department of Social Services. I am so thankful for everything she did for us. She was my hero. She also was the first person who introduced me to my Heavenly Father. She was not a regular churchgoing person, but she was a regular Biblereading person who had a deep faith. She taught me that despite all that had happened, my life was in the hands of my Heavenly Father who loved me and would always be with me. She taught me how to forgive and extend grace to those who had hurt me. She taught me how to *love*.

In 1977, I had planned to return to North Carolina for the first time since we left. I wanted to see my Aunt Edna. However, I did not make it in time. She had passed away. The biggest regret I have in my entire life is that I did not get to see her and thank her for everything she did for me before she was called home by our Father. I did go back to North Carolina for her funeral, but I could not bring myself to attend. The pain of loss for me was so strong that I was an emotional wreck. However, I know that one day we will meet again face to face, and I will be able to tell her how much I loved her and how thankful I am for all she did for me.

The Virginia Years

When my mother came to North Carolina in 1962 to take the remainder of us back to Virginia my Heavenly Father brought John Caldwell into my life. My mom had met John after she moved to Virginia. John was a quiet, unassuming man who was raised in the hills of West Virginia. He had enlisted in the Navy in his teens and become an engineman, working on the motors and engines of various ships he was on. Not long after my mom and John met, they decided to marry. My mom sometimes fell asleep crying in his arms, telling him how much she missed her children. Over the next year, he encouraged her to go to North Carolina and bring us back to Virginia. He could have easily said he did not sign up for the responsibility of seven children, but instead he did the exact opposite—he embraced us.

John knew what I had gone through in North Carolina and how much my biological father had hurt me physically, mentally, and emotionally. For two years after I moved to Virginia, John demonstrated what a real man and father was all about. He often talked to me about my experiences and how my biological father was neither a man nor a father nor a husband. He shared the day-to-day demands of caring for and raising children, let alone seven of them.

He was my first role model of what a real man should be. He truly was my dad.

After two years in Virginia, I met a young man and married him in 1964 when I was 16. At the time, I thought he would be for me what my stepdad was for my mother. During the early years of our marriage, he embraced my family, and we spent a great deal of time with them. We often talked about having children, but over the next five years, I was not able to conceive. In 1969, after a period of suffering continual pain, I was diagnosed with a chronic infection in both my legs. The doctors treated the infection with various antibiotics to no avail. I was repeatedly hospitalized over the next year or so, but the infection continued to get worse. After attempting a variety of treatments and procedures to fight the infection, my team of doctors told me I had no choice. Due to the extreme level of physical and sexual abuse I had suffered, a complete hysterectomy was my only option. So in 1970, my ability to have my own children was forever removed from me.

When the medical staff wheeled me into the operating room to perform the surgery, I had a sensation that went through my entire body. It was a warm, loving feeling, and I knew right then that everything would be okay. I no longer had anything to fear. My mother, who was by my side, was crying. I told her, "Don't worry. I am going to be okay." Since then, my Heavenly Father has walked beside me every day, no matter what. He periodically gives me visions of what is to come, and they always come to pass. It truly is a gift from Him.

Not long after the surgery, I began to lose weight and have severe abdominal pain. That went on for months before I was again hospitalized. The doctors found a tumor lodged between my kidneys and bladder. It was not visible on the X-rays that were taken, but the doctors could feel it. They believed the tumor was a residual piece of the original infection that had grown into a tumor. The end result was that I had to have another surgery to remove this tumor.

During the years when I was dealing with my medical experiences, I drew closer to my Heavenly Father. I talked with Him every day, asking Him to give me strength to handle the pain and to give me healing. I also developed a desire to become more independent and able to support myself. So I made a life-changing decision to enroll in cosmetology school and become a hair stylist. During the early to mid-1970s, the combination of my medical experiences, my faith, and my ability to earn an income led me in a different direction than what my husband wanted. I prayed regularly about what to do. I tried repeatedly to bring us closer together, but as time progressed, we continued to drift farther apart. I did not want to disrupt the family relationships he had with members of my family, particularly my brothers, and I was not sure I could make it on my own. However, my Heavenly Father, as He did when I had the hysterectomy, embraced me and let me know He would always be there next to me. He would carry me when necessary. He made sure I knew that *He had this.*

In 1977, after 13 years of marriage, I moved out of our house. I rented a one-bedroom apartment and gave the house we owned to my husband. This was the first time in my life I had been totally on my own. No one else lived with me, and no one supported me financially. Some members of my family were not happy with my decision. The family life they had known up to that time was no more. While my ex-husband continues to have relationships with some of my family members, never again were the family gatherings the same as they had been.

God's Plan

After moving out on my own in 1977, I met a man named Randy who was in the Navy. He came to the salon where I worked to have his hair cut. We got to know each other and eventually went out on a few dates. One time when we were dating, Randy suggested we double-date with a friend of his named Ray. We did, and as a result, I met Mary. Ray and Mary were both in the Navy. Mary was raised in the Philadelphia—South Jersey area. After graduating from high school, she went to college for one year before running out of money. As a result, she enlisted in the Navy and was stationed in Norfolk, Virginia, where she met Ray.

Over the next few months, Mary and I developed a close friendship. Randy disappeared out of my life, but Mary and I became very close. Although she had her relationship with Ray, this was the first time in both our lives we were totally responsible for ourselves. We were able to talk with each other like sisters. At the time, two of my sisters lived in other parts of the country, and my other sister was busy raising her children.

As time progressed, Mary and Ray decided to get married. Mary asked me to be her maid of honor, which I was glad to do. Ray asked Mary's older brother to be his best man. Her brother accepted and then asked to meet the maid of honor before spending a weekend together at the wedding. Thus Bob Marshall came into my life. Bob, who lived in North Jersey and worked in New York City as a CPA, came to Virginia on vacation in August 1977. He spent most of his time with Mary and Ray, but they brought him to the salon one afternoon to meet me. All of us talked briefly and then decided to have dinner and go dancing on Saturday evening. None of us considered it a date—just a chance to get to know each other. After all, Bob was dating someone back in New Jersey.

Mary and Ray's wedding was in October in South Jersey where Mary had spent the latter years of her childhood. We all celebrated their wedding, and Bob and I got to know more about each other. After the wedding, Mary, Ray, and I went back to Norfolk, and Bob returned to North Jersey. A few months later in February 1978, Mary asked me to go to South Jersey with her to visit her mother and stepfather for a weekend. At the wedding, I had come to like her mother and stepfather, so I said sure. Little did I know that once Bob found out I was coming to South Jersey, he drove down from North Jersey for the weekend. There were still no dates, but all of us spent the weekend laughing, talking, sharing, and having good family time. I did not know until later that Bob broke up with the girl he was dating after that weekend.

In May, Ray and Mary suggested that we spend Memorial Day weekend at King's Dominion amusement park outside Richmond, Virginia. I thought it would be fun, so I said yes. Once I said yes, Mary called Bob and invited him to come. Mary and I shared one hotel room, and Ray and Bob shared another. We had a fun weekend, and that was the first time Bob and I kissed. We both knew something was beginning to happen.

In June, when Mary was eight months pregnant with her first son, she moved into my apartment with me because Ray had to go on temporary deployment. For the next few weeks, we lived together. One time while sunning ourselves by the pool, I went into what I thought was the shallow end. I immediately realized it was the deep end and began to struggle since I had never learned to swim. Mary was eight months pregnant, but she and a bystander jumped in to rescue me.

Shortly after the pool episode, hoping Ray would be home from temporary deployment by then, we decided to go to Busch Gardens amusement park for the July 4th weekend. However, as it turned out, Ray was not able to come home, and due to the proximity of Mary's due date and condition, she went back to New Jersey to be with her mother and stepfather while awaiting the delivery of her first child at Philadelphia Naval Hospital. When I left work to come home the day before the holiday, I found Bob Marshall standing next to his powder blue Camaro in my parking lot. I did not realize he was still planning to come to Virginia after things worked out the way they did with Mary and Ray. I had to decide what to do. We talked, and I agreed to still go to Busch Gardens with him. I told him he could sleep on my couch for the weekend but nothing more. He was fine with that. The next day, we spent the entire day at Busch Gardens, riding the Loch Ness monster and other rides, seeing shows, eating, and having a great time together.

Little did either of us realize that this weekend together would become the beginning of a two-year, long-distance relationship—me in Virginia and him in North Jersey. Over the next two years, Bob often drove down from New Jersey on a Friday evening and drove back home on Sunday night—a six-hour drive each way. He sometimes managed to get audit assignments for clients in Southeast Virginia so he could spend days and sometimes weeks at a time with me. For two years, we spent every holiday and as much time as possible together. On Saturday nights, if he was not in Virginia with me, he called me on the phone just as the TV show *Love Boat* was ending, and we would talk for an hour or more. That was back in the day when it was an expensive toll call.

Our love for each other was the most intense and passionate love I had ever felt. We knew we wanted to be together for the rest of our lives, so on July 13, 1980, we exchanged vows at the altar of Christ Lutheran Church in Norfolk. My one and only earthly father, John Caldwell, walked me down the aisle and brought me to the hand of the one and only man I would spend the rest of my life with. When we exchanged vows, we deleted the words *'til death do us part*. Instead, we substituted the words *always and forever*. On that day, we affirmed to each other that we would love, honor, and cherish each other always and forever. We both understood what those words meant. There would never be another—only each of us for the other.

Over the subsequent years, we often looked back on all the events that had to occur in order for us to meet and marry. What are the odds of a Lumbee Indian farmgirl from the depths of North Carolina meeting and marrying a poor white kid who grew up in a South Philadelphia row house? Only our Heavenly Father could have planned and orchestrated it. There simply is no other explanation.

The Yuppie Years

Despite our love for each other, the first 10 years of our marriage were undoubtedly the most difficult years for me. One of Bob's driving factors was his steadfast desire to never return to the poverty he had experienced growing up in South Philadelphia. Bob's parents had never graduated from high school. His mother was 17 and his father was 19 when they ran away to Maryland and got married in December 1953. Ten months later, four days after his mother turned 18, Bob was born. About two years later, his sister, Mary, was born. For the first two years of Bob's life, they lived with his father's parents, grandparent, and younger brother in West Philadelphia. After his sister was born, they moved to a South Philadelphia row house. Over the next 11 years, they lived in three different houses on the same small street in South Philly. His father worked for a minimal paycheck while his mother raised him and his sister.

When Bob was eight years old, his third-grade teacher saw a great deal of educational potential in him and was able to arrange for him to attend the Masterman School in Philadelphia, a school for gifted children. Over the next few years, Bob attended school with children of all races and socioeconomic backgrounds. While some classmates were as poor as he was, there were also children whose parents were doctors, lawyers, and other professionals. He often said later in his adult life that the ability to see and experience an entirely different world than anything he had seen before totally changed him. Had it not been for this opportunity, he most likely would have ended up in jail or dead, which happens to so many children who grow up in his original environment.

In 1963 when Bob was nine years old, his father was diagnosed with an aggressive strain of multiple sclerosis. His father could no longer work, so his mother had to get a job to support them. Over the next four years, his father's condition deteriorated, and the pressures on his mother increased. She reached a point where she could no longer handle it. One night between Christmas and New Year's in 1967, his mother sat down with her husband, her children, Bob, and Mary and told them she was leaving. She gave them a choice—stay in Philly with their father or move to South Jersey with her. Bob chose to stay with his father, and Mary went with their mother and moved to South Jersey to live with her and the man who later became their stepfather. Bob's father's condition left him in a wheelchair, a bed, and a hospital. Bob became the primary caregiver even though he was only 13 years old.

He cleaned his father's catheter bag, tube, and bedpan. He bathed him, prepared food, fed him, gave him his shots, and did whatever else he needed to do. Bob's education suffered, and he almost failed the ninth grade due to excessive absences. Even though Bob had help from his father's mother who lived around the corner and some of the neighbors, he was primarily responsible for his father's care. Whenever his father was hospitalized, Bob's Aunt Dot and Uncle Jack would pick Bob up from Central High School on Fridays and take him to their house in New Jersey for the weekend. Then they would drive him back to school on Monday morning. Six months after Bob's mother moved out, his father died from the effects of MS, and Bob had to move in with his mother and now stepfather in South Jersey.

Little did Bob know how these caregiving experiences would lay the foundation for events later in his life. They would instill in Bob an intense drive to accumulate significant financial resources so he would never have to endure what he had experienced as a child. Enough would never be enough. He was the classic Yuppie. During the first 10 years of our marriage, we had a six-figure income.

We bought and lived in three different houses, each one bigger and better than the previous one. We had nice things and multiple cars. We traveled places and reaped the financial reward of Bob's efforts. However, there was a price to be paid. He was so intent on climbing the ladder of success that he sacrificed his values to do so. He was frequently out late at night with his boss, drinking and doing what it took to succeed in the corporate world. I cannot begin to count how many evenings I prayed and prayed to our Heavenly Father for Bob—to keep him safe, bring him home unharmed, not let him hurt anyone, and change his ways.

During these first few years, Bob and I made a life-changing decision. He knew I could not give birth to children. We had talked during our courtship about adopting children after we were married, but then we decided that with our other priorities, we could not devote the time and attention to a child that he or she deserved. So instead, we decided to focus on our nieces and nephews—27 between the two of us. For many of our brothers and sisters, education was not a priority, and the environment they were raising their children in was less than ideal. We decided to focus on making a difference in as many of their lives as we could. We wanted to be their role models, take them on trips to various places they would not otherwise have gone, and have them spend time at our house. We encouraged them to get a quality education and achieve whatever success they chose.

Another thing we did during those 10 years was join the Jaycees (Junior Chamber of Commerce), a young person's (under 40) leadership development and civic training organization. Like his work life, Bob was intensely dedicated to that organization. He spent a great deal of time in leadership and managing projects designed to benefit those in need. His drive to both succeed and make a difference in someone else's life fueled his efforts. We were blessed to meet many people, both in the organization and the community. We developed relationships that have continued to this day.

Another significant event during this time was the death of my father, John Caldwell, in March 1986 from asbestosis. He truly was my father in every way. He demonstrated what a true father should be like. I will be eternally grateful to him, and I know we will meet again.

The True Love Years

When Bob was a child in South Philly, he and his sister walked three city blocks to Sunday school. He learned a lot about Christianity, but he did not have *faith*. When he moved to South Jersey and later in college, his connection with church ceased. When he met me, he began to learn what faith was all about but did not want to attend church or truly give his life to Christ. During our first 10 years, we did not regularly attend church. He would usually only go with me on Christmas and Easter.

Despite Bob's reluctance, God always has a way of getting our attention and implementing His plan for us. In late 1989, the parent corporation of the real estate development company Bob worked for decided to get out of the business. That totally upset the world Bob knew and introduced an element of uncertainty to his life. He did not know what to do. That uncertainty brought him to his knees and made him realize that anything he achieved was not of his doing but rather because of God's doing. Everything could easily be taken away. When Bob truly recognized that in January 1990, he accepted the Lord as his personal Savior, and we began to regularly attend church. Bob began to experience personal growth in his faith. However, he still had some unfinished business. For a year and eight months after he lost his job, he and his former boss did some homebuilding together, but Bob realized he would never be able to be true to his faith if he continued to partner with this person. So in September 1992, Bob began his own design and homebuilding company.

Once again, our Heavenly Father had a plan. When Bob partnered with his former boss, he was blessed to be introduced to a man, Allan, who was 18 years his senior. He was a wealthy local dentist who often invested in real estate. What Bob did not know at first was that although Allan was of the Jewish faith, he had a deep, battle-tested faith that was the result of his very own personal struggles, including alcoholism. He had been sober for a number of years and regularly attended Alcoholics Anonymous (AA) meetings and sponsored other alcoholics. Allan quickly became a mentor and father-like figure to Bob. He was a genuine, honest individual who wielded great influence and earned Bob's respect. Allan saw the potential in Bob and agreed to become his business partner in the homebuilding business. Thirty-two years later, they still do business together, speak on a regular basis, and support each other when times get difficult. Only because of our Father's blessing and plan did this happen.

Bob was not the only one our Father had a business plan for. In early 1997, I began to feel it was time for me to move on in my professional career. I had been at the same salon for a number of years and had developed close, personal relationships with the women I worked with. We were like sisters, not just coworkers, but I believed our Father was telling me to start looking at alternatives. For a few months I explored other salons, and in May 1997, I found a salon I felt comfortable with. The owner and I discussed the specifics. I gave my notice at the salon where I had been working, but I just could not complete the process of starting the new position. I felt that our Father was still telling me to continue looking. A couple weeks later, a friend of mine at church asked me if I was still looking for a new position.

When I said yes, she told me that the salon she went to about 2 miles from my house was for sale. It was a large salon with 10 stylists, two nail technicians, and four receptionists. Even though I lived close by, I had never noticed the salon. I went to see the salon before contacting the owner. The minute I laid eyes on the salon, I *knew* it was where my Father wanted me to be. The name of the salon was Marshall's Hair Design. How else could anyone explain that the salon was already named after me before I ever set foot in it? It simply had to be where my Father wanted me to be. The end result was that on July 7, 1997, I became the legal owner of Marshall's Hair Design.

I always viewed the salon as a gift from my Heavenly Father. With that gift came a responsibility—to use that gift to benefit others. Over the years, many people—clients and staff—came into the salon. Some were hurting. Some did not know my Heavenly Father. Some had experienced horrendous events in their lives just as I had. Marshall's Hair Design became my place of ministry. I tried to inspire people, share my faith, and show them genuine compassion and love. We took donations and provided food and clothing for people in need. We often held events to raise money for charities that focused on meeting people's needs. Marshall's was a place where the glory of God shone brightly, where people over time left in a better place than they were when they first came in. I was also blessed to have Bob help me. His business background helped me learn things I did not know about the financial and management side of business. Even though I owned Marshall's, Bob was a vital contributor to both the business and the faith side of it. Many Saturday evenings, the two of us were at the salon until 8:00 p.m. or later handling the business affairs.

It was during these years of our marriage that our *love* for each other grew to a strong, mature level. We truly were there for each other. I cannot imagine ever experiencing a greater love in the fullest sense of the word than during those times. On Valentine's Day 2004, Bob gave me a valentine that I still have and will cherish forever. It was heartfelt and written word for word by him to me. It read as follows:

> Rather than buy a card with preprinted words on it, this Valentine's Day I wanted to take the time to put my own words on paper, to tell you what you mean to me.
>
> First, you are my *rock*. I know that you are always there for me, to strengthen me, to comfort me, to guide me, and to love me. I know that I can always depend upon you.
>
> Even if we don't agree on something, we can always work things out, and you will still be there for me.
>
> Second, you are my *inspiration*. You are the kindest, gentlest, most sincere, and loving person I have ever known. No matter what anyone may do to you, you still show kind words and understanding to them. You constantly try to find the good in people and make allowances for the bad. You try not to judge people because you know full well that it could just as easily be you in their shoes.
>
> Third, you are the source of my *faith*. Were it not for you, I would still be lost in the wilderness. Because of you, I have found my faith and have a relationship with God. While I can only aspire to reach the level of faith you have, I continue to try to improve and grow my own faith because of you. We have always said that God put us together.

Fourth, you are my *passion*. You have always been able to make me feel and experience things that most people can only dream of. The love we share generates the physical feelings in us that are beyond belief. The excitement, the joy, the sensations are simply the best anyone could ever hope for.

Fifth, you are my *wife and best friend*. We confide in each other; you pick me up when I'm down and help me through the rough times in life. Through good times and bad, you support me and care for me. When other men at church talk about needing an "accountability partner," I think to myself that I already have the best partner any man could ever hope for and that I will always be accountable to you.

Lastly, you are my *love*. What I feel for you is something that I have never felt at any other time in my life. I would give my life to save you if I had to. You are the most important aspect of my life on this earth, and I cannot imagine living without you. All else in my life is secondary to you and how I feel about you. I will always love you and cherish what we have.

May God bless you this Valentine's Day! All my love *forever and always*, Baby.

During these same years, my relationship with my mother changed. She had received a large financial settlement due to the death of my father, John, from asbestosis. Those funds were her only source of income other than Social Security. Given her lack of education, particularly of a financial nature, some family members and people around her took advantage of her. They convinced her to give them money to pay for a house, a car, and other items. In addition, my mother was in the beginning stages of dementia and not fully aware of her surroundings or the people around her. After a couple years of this, my sister Marie and I stepped in. After various confrontations with those involved, we hired attorneys and went to court. I was appointed my mother's legal guardian with a full power of attorney for her assets and affairs.

Over the next approximately 10 years, my sister and I managed all my mother's affairs. We took control of her funds and placed them in a trust for her benefit. We handled the repairs and eventual sale of her house, with all the proceeds being added to the trust. We moved her into an assisted living facility at first. As she progressed through the various stages of dementia, we eventually had to move her from the assisted living facility to a home for senior citizens with dementia. Her condition worsened as time progressed. Eventually she was unable to speak or control her body movements. She was completely unaware of anyone or anything around her. Nearly every Tuesday afternoon, Marie and I went to see Mom. We spent time with her, bathed her, fed her, dressed her, and sometimes took her for a ride so she could have some time away from the facility. Occasionally on holidays, we brought her to one of our houses to spend time with family, even though for the most part she did not know anyone and was unable to communicate with us. In December 2006, Mom died. My last contribution to her was handling the sale and distribution of her assets in accordance with her Last Will and Testament. Although my mother had once abandoned all her children, it would have been easy for me to have anger toward her for the rest of my life. However, that was not the case. My Heavenly Father taught me how to forgive and extend grace—how to really *love*. I loved my mother throughout all my adult years. I have no regrets for taking responsibility for her during the last years of her life. I would gladly do it again.

The Beginning of a New Life

During the five or six years after my mother died, Bob and I experienced some changes—changes that would have a significant impact on our lives.

First, the existing lease for the salon expired in 2007. Despite our requests for a new or extended lease, we ended up renting month to month until the latter part of 2008 when the landlord gave us notice to vacate the premises. They were going to combine our space and the one next to us and open a liquor store. They gave us the opportunity to lease another space in the shopping center, but none of the spaces were suited for our operation. Any of them would have required a complete remodel to accommodate our furnishings and equipment, particularly the plumbing. A remodel would have cost approximately $100,000 or more and put us in a significantly worse location in the shopping center. Bob and I decided it was not worth doing and that we would simply close the salon. However, that was not our Father's plan. When we discussed this with the employees, every one of them wanted to remain together and encouraged us to find another location in a different shopping center. After much prayer, I began seeking other alternatives.

I looked at a new shopping center under construction, one I had looked at before but felt it was too expensive. I met with the leasing agent and saw the available spaces. The agent said the rent the Landlord was asking for had been significantly reduced. The Landlord was willing to lease us a better, more centralized space at approximately half the rent mentioned previously. In addition, the first six months would be rent-free, which would help us build out the space while we were not paying rent. Further, they were willing to lease us a 1,600 square foot space and only charge us rent for a 1,200 square foot space during the entire lease term. The agent also said it would be about three or four months before their construction would be far enough along for us to take possession of the empty shell and begin our internal construction, which would probably take three or four additional months. If we were to take this space, what would we do with our employees in the meantime? Well, it turned out that there was another salon in our current shopping center that had significant available space. One of my employees knew one of theirs, conversations occurred, and I was able to rent enough chairs in this woman's salon to accommodate all my employees. I had to find space for myself in another salon nearby, which I was able to do. The end result was that all of us would be able to continue working while our new shopping center was finishing construction.

The second issue was the construction schedule. While there was little I could do to accelerate the schedule, thanks to Bob and his staff, we could fast track the internal construction portion. Bob and his staff did the complete design and approved plans and then the actual construction. The Landlord turned the space over to us on March 23, 2009. Bob and his staff completed the internal construction in late June, and we had our grand opening on June 23, 2009. The salon is still located in this space.

None of this would have been possible if it were not for our Heavenly Father. As always, many things occur that cannot be explained in any other way. His time—His plan.

Another change that occurred was the church we attended. We had been members of a local Baptist church since 2002. Due to some internal church issues, Bob felt led to explore other churches. I was not ready to leave, but in 2007, Bob attended services at several other churches. He eventually attended another Baptist church for about six months. We went to Christmas services there, and Bob joined the choir. But he was still not comfortable and felt led to continue seeking a different church home. After a couple months, I happened to mention to a friend of ours that we were once again seeking a church home. He mentioned that he and his wife had recently changed churches and begun attending New Life Church. It was a multicultural, multiservice, charismatic worship church that began approximately 10 years earlier and had grown to about 2,000 members. We decided to attend a service and see what it was like. On September 13, 2009, Bob and I attended our first service at New Life. We both knew when the service was over that we had found our home. Our Father had brought us where we were supposed to be. To this day, we continue to be members and leaders of New Life, a church that now has five campuses with over 5,000 members and continues to bring our Father's love to those who do not yet know Him.

About a year after we joined New Life, we joined a life group our friends led. The group consisted of 10 to 14 people and met twice a month to pray, study, and fellowship. Over time we built personal relationships with the people in the group, relationships where we could share our innermost feelings and thoughts. Over the latter half of 2011, Bob began to feel that he was being led away from his business and into some form of ministry. He discussed these feelings with members of the group, seeking guidance and prayer. During that time, a woman from Australia who traveled the world evangelizing attended one of our meetings. She had the spiritual gift of prophecy. She asked to lay hands on each person and share with them what she saw from our Father. Bob was not quite ready to embrace this, but I was. When she laid hands on me, she said, "Quit fighting. The Lord is going to do something with you, and people are going to marvel at it." I had no idea what she was talking about. I did not understand what she was telling me. The amazing part was that she was telling me that the good Lord was going to do something with me.

As time passed, Bob felt more and more that the Lord was telling him to leave his business and begin a new life in God's service. At the end of 2011, Bob began to wind down his construction activities. Over the next few months, he became more active in ministry at church. He became one of the teachers for a special needs children's Sunday school class. He joined the Kids' Hope program that provides mentors to elementary school children from impoverished, at-risk home environments. I became a Sunday school teacher for two- and three-year-old children.

Most significantly, Bob was invited to become part of a missions team that was going to India for two weeks in May. That trip forever left a lasting impression on him. The team traveled to New Delhi where it had the opportunity to visit a Christian school in the heart of the slums immediately outside the city. The team then traveled to the northern Punjab region of India adjacent to the Pakistani border where they spent about 10 days at a Christian orphanage operated by our church's missionaries. The team led events for the children at the orphanage and children from surrounding villages. In the evenings, the team traveled to nearby villages and led services.

When Bob returned home from India, he shared the abject

poverty and abysmal living conditions that he saw. Even today, the memories of that trip are seared into his heart and soul. Bob returned home from India on May 22, 2012. On July 17, 2012, our Father revealed His plans for us, and we began our new life.

Day 1 PC (Post Cancer)
Facing New Days

July 17, 2012

At 9:30 am on Tuesday, July 17, 2012, Bob and I met with our family doctor. I had been experiencing severe abdominal pain and difficulty moving my bowels over the past few weeks. After several tests, including a CT scan, I came home on Friday afternoon to a message on our answering machine from our family doctor that said, "Please come to our office on Tuesday morning, and bring your husband with you." Over the next few days I did not know what he wanted to discuss, but I knew it could not be good.

On Tuesday morning, the doctor told us I had cancer. A good-sized tumor in my colon was restricting normal bowel movements, and various smaller tumors were on my liver and lower lungs. That day was the beginning of facing new days. One day I was working without any symptoms, and the next day I find out I have a life-threatening disease. That day our lives became a new journey. The life we had come to know was *gone*.

While we were still at the doctor's office, the doctor consulted with an oncologist and a surgeon. During the phone calls, I remember telling Bob that I wanted to "run like a horse." The consensus of the three professionals was to admit me to a local hospital for surgery.

At 3:30 p.m., we met with the surgeon who was to perform the operation. He said he had a cancellation that afternoon, so he could perform the surgery. Later we found out that he was a devout Christian who often traveled on medical evangelistic missions.

At 4:15 p.m., they wheeled me into the operating room. They put me under anesthesia and began the surgery. It was during this time that Jesus came to me. He was waist-deep in a pool of frothing, swirling mud. He was dressed in clothes that a construction worker would wear. He had a three-day beard and shoulder-length, curly, wavy hair. He was toting what looked like a heavy, full duffel bag over His shoulder.

As Jesus continued stomping through the mud, He said to me, "Don't worry, Mildred. *I've got this.*"

The surgery was finished at 7:00 p.m. The surgeon came out and told Bob I had Stage 4 colon cancer. He had to remove a significant portion of my colon but was able to leave enough to avoid a colostomy bag being attached to my body. He also removed several smaller tumors on my liver and the lower portions of my lungs. Nine of the 14 lymph nodes he removed showed signs of cancer. He was 99 percent sure that everything was cancerous but would wait until the pathology report came back to know for sure. He told Bob, "Get her affairs in order. She will be lucky to live two years."

At 9:00 p.m. I was wheeled out of the surgical recovery area. As I was on my way to my room, my sister and sister-in-law heard me reciting the 23rd Psalm—"The Lord is my Shepherd . . ." They came over to me, held my hands, and helped me recite it. I was awake most of the night hollering for pain medicine since they had cut open a significant portion of my abdominal cavity.

The remainder of the story consists of real-time, as-they-happened posts written by Bob on Mildred's CaringBridge site.'

Day 2 PC
Bob's Perspective

July 19, 2012

As Mildred and I begin this new journey in our life, please know that we are at peace with whatever happens. While we certainly would prefer that all evidence of the cancer disappear from her body, we know that our God is with us and will provide the strength necessary to deal with anything we encounter. One of the true tests of faith is our ability to accept without reservation God's will being done, even when it is different from our will. We have no doubt that He will walk this path with us. We are often comforted by the poem called "Footprints" that I am sure most of you are familiar with. When there is only one set of footprints in the sand, that is when He is carrying us. We covet each of your prayers but simply ask that you pray He gives us the strength to complete this new journey, however long it may be. We thank each of you for being part of our lives. May God bless you as we go forward.

Day 4 PC
Post-Surgery

July 21, 2012

Mere words are inadequate to describe the outpouring of love and support we have received from each of you. Today was a good day since it was better than yesterday, and hopefully tomorrow will be better than today. Mildred was able to take four walks of a slightly longer distance and then sit in the recliner for 30 minutes after the first three walks. She sat in the chair for most of this evening, approximately three hours, before getting back into bed. She was more alert than previous days and slept off and on during the day.

We are still focusing on her return home, probably Monday or Tuesday, but we will know more over the weekend. The incision appears to be healing properly. The largest hurdle at the moment is for her to pass gas. Until that happens, she still can only drink water or apple juice. According to the surgeon, she should be able to do so this weekend, based on normal time frames for this type of surgery. This is necessary to demonstrate that everything is working properly in her colon, and it must happen before reintroducing solid foods to her system. Even then, she will only be able to eat soft foods such as Jell-O, pudding, light soups, and such until she has a normal bowel movement, which will probably be a few days after passing gas.

God continues to surround her with His angels. We found out tonight that the nurse (Bernadette) who has been attending to her the last four days from 7:00 p.m. to 7:00 a.m. is a client of Mildred's salon. Bernadette was not used to seeing Mildred in such rough shape, and thus it took a while for her to recognize Mildred. In addition, an old friend (Holly) from our first church was one of the night nurses on her floor tonight and will be over the weekend. And the nurse (Vickie) who ran the group home where Mildred's mother stayed the last 10 years of her life was one of the nurses on the adjacent hall. I have no doubt that God will continue to wrap her in His loving arms and take care of her. I know we will win this battle with God's presence alongside us and the love of each of you. I look forward to the day when Mildred can stand before all and give God the glory for the miracle He has worked in her.

Day 5 PC

Forward Steps

July 22, 2012

Today was another day in what I hope will be small steps forward. Mildred was able to walk a little farther and more frequently than Friday. She was able to sit up in the chair after each walk for longer periods of time. Most importantly, she passed gas. I never thought I would be so happy to hear someone pass gas, but it sure was a momentous event for her. Tomorrow she should be able to eat soft foods. Once they work through her system so she can have a normal bowel movement, she can begin eating solid foods. Although we have not yet had the conversation with the surgeon about what she will be able to eat when she leaves the hospital, I suspect her diet will change to less rich, blander foods to minimize the impact on her system. She was awake for longer periods of time and more alert today than yesterday. So once again, a small step forward.

Again, we cannot begin to thank each of you enough for the support, love, and, most of all, prayers. She has an army of prayer warriors that stretches from the West Coast (California, Oregon) to the East Coast (Florida to Massachusetts), and from Michigan in the north to Texas down south. We could never have imagined that so many people in so many places would lift her up in prayer to our God. It is truly an incredible blessing.

May our God continue to rain down his healing powers on Mildred and give her the strength to continue this new journey in life. I know He will be beside us every step we take.

Day 6 PC

A Good Day

July 23, 2012

Today was a really good day for Mildred. She alternated between sitting upright in the chair and lying on the bed in a semi-upright position throughout the entire day. She had a steady stream of visitors who helped give her more strength. She truly enjoyed seeing everyone and the love they expressed to her. I know this is repetitive, but we cannot thank each of you enough for the love and support you have given us. We are truly blessed to be surrounded by friends and loved ones such as yourselves. Mildred also was able to walk from one end of the hall to the other and back. She ate soft foods for lunch and dinner.

While today was a good day, I harbor no illusions about the length and difficulty of this journey. The first phase of the journey, her hospitalization, is coming to an end. Phase two, her recovery from the surgery, will cover the next six weeks, and then we begin the most difficult phase—chemotherapy. I expect to have more good days than bad, but I also know we will overcome the bad days and successfully complete this journey. I have been blessed to have Mildred as part of my life for 34 years. During that time, she has given me more than I ever deserved in support, love, and care. Now it is time for me to give back to her what she has so freely given me. With God leading the way, I know we will succeed. We thank each of you for your continued prayers and love.

Day 9 PC

Home

July 26, 2012

Mildred has spent the last two days at home, resting and walking laps around our deck. The doctors want her to walk four to five times a day while she recovers. She still tires more than normal but is getting a little more energy each day. She is eating okay, and we continue to be blessed with food from friends and loved ones. It's a good thing since I am not a cook by any definition. Mildred is scheduled to see the surgeon on Monday, and hopefully they will remove the staples and sutures. Then we will meet with the oncologist to discuss her case and proposed treatments.

The most difficult aspect right now is her mental ability to accept what has happened and the chemo going forward. All of this has occurred in the span of nine days, and it seems surreal to her. She is trying to come to grips with the fact that she really does have cancer and what all that means going forward. We continue to seek God's wisdom and strength in all of this. Hopefully, He will guide her to the place where she can begin some productive treatment.

We continue to be so thankful for all your prayers and the network of prayer warriors you have connected with that we do not even know about. His strength continues to flow through our bodies as a result of the efforts of each of you. Thank you again.

Day 17 PC

Roller Coaster Week

August 3, 2012

This past week has probably been the introduction for how life from here on will be—a week of highs and lows. On Monday, July 30th, we met with the surgeon to remove the staples and sutures. He reviewed the pathology report with us, which confirmed that the tumors on the liver were cancerous. Of the 14 lymph nodes he removed, nine were cancerous. The report confirmed her status as Stage 4. He said there was no way right now that the cancer can be cured; it can only be controlled. In order to totally remove the cancer, assuming they got it all in the colon, he would have to remove 90 percent of her liver and one of her lungs.

Obviously, that's not a condition in which the human body can function. Since Mildred already has cancer, she is not a candidate for a transplant. If chemotherapy reduces the size and growth rate of the remaining tumors, it will buy her some time and quality of life. In his opinion, with successful chemo, she could live two years—three if she is fortunate. Clearly, this was the low point of the week.

On Thursday, we met with the oncologist, Dr. Steinberg of Virginia Oncology Associates (VOA). I read his bio before we met and thought I would like him because he was born and raised in New York City, went to college and med school at New York University, and served on the staff of Sloan Kettering Cancer Institute before joining VOA in 1982. I was hoping he would have a typical NYC attitude of "can do, no matter what the obstacles," and that is exactly what he has. He discussed the tests, scans, and more that have already been performed and confirmed that Mildred has Stage 4 and it cannot be cured. However, he said he does believe that successful treatment will allow her to live a productive life. He encourages his patients not to get caught up in a pity party but rather go out and live life to the fullest each day as if they did not have cancer. His recommended treatment is to immediately begin the FOLFOX chemo regimen that has six drugs given every other week for 12 weeks. She will undergo a PET scan next week to establish a baseline image and status, and then another scan after the six treatments for comparison purposes. If the treatments are successful in reducing the size of the tumors, she will continue the FOLFOX regimen for another six treatments and then see where she is at. If the tumors have not been reduced after six treatments, he will consult with his colleagues at Duke University to enroll her in a clinical trial. While he stated that he is not God, he does believe that two or three years is at the low end of possibilities. Five or six years is more likely if she is willing to be flexible in how the cancer is treated. And she might even make 10 years. She is scheduled to begin the first chemo treatment on Monday, August 13th and continue every other week for five more treatments, ending on October 22nd.

While our hopes at the beginning of the week were depressed by the negative outlook and we were reduced to praying for a miracle, we now feel that we are in the fight. We know God has this in His control. While that does not mean He will make it turn out exactly as we want, we do believe He has sent us a doctor who will do everything he knows how to do to successfully control this disease. I, too, will put every ounce of strength I have into this battle. While the final outcome is unknown to us, we will celebrate the life God has given us and live it to the fullest each day. Tim McGraw's song "Live Every Day Like You Were Dying" exemplifies what our life will be like for however long God chooses to give us.

Day 24 PC

A Challenging Week

August 9, 2012

Mildred has had a challenging week. The early part of the week she battled constipation, which could have posed serious problems. After taking a couple different laxatives, her surgeon's nurse prescribed a magnesia—prune juice mix that solved the problem.

Earlier today, Mildred had outpatient surgery to implant a port device under her skin and connect it to a vein in her neck. The surgery went well, and she is now home resting again. The oncologist will use the port to connect her chemo treatments and infuse the drugs directly into her veins. She is still scheduled for her first treatment on Monday, August 13th.

This journey would be a great deal more difficult if it were not for each of you and the strength our God continues to impart to us. We are thankful and find joy in each and every day. The visits of so many of you continue to lift her spirits. We pray that as she begins the chemo treatments, they will not overwhelm her with the side effects we have read about. The oncologist has already given her two prescriptions to counteract the potential side effects, but we hope they will not be necessary. We continue to look to the Great Physician in this process and ask for His healing and strength.

In The Words of Mildred

KELLO

My Heavenly Father has a good sense of humor about what I have been through up until now. About a week or two after I came home from the hospital, I received a card in the mail. My Heavenly Father had used one of the ladies I went to Bible study with for 12 and a half years to send me a message. Her name was Betty. She could not see due to a degenerative eye disease along with glaucoma. The card she sent me had the most beautiful horse on it, mostly white with a little gray. The card read, "As you face new days . . ." When I received the card, I screamed and cried. I experienced all the emotions in the human body because I felt like that was my redemption. My Heavenly Father was once again telling me, "I've got this." Betty had no idea that the card she sent had a horse on it. Her husband actually picked out the card for her. Later, when I went to church and our pastoral and elder staff laid hands on me and prayed for me, I was told that a horse was a sign of strength. What an amazing day that was!

Day 28 PC

Strength of Faith

August 13, 2012

While Mildred continues to physically heal from her surgeries, she still does not have the energy level she had before. She has been doing walking exercises on a daily basis and has gone to the salon to visit clients and employees. She is usually tired and ready for bed by 10:00 p.m. Her balance is still slightly unsteady, and she continues to use a walking cane for assistance. I continue to pray that God will restore her physical strength so she is able to wage this battle. Her strength of faith, as it has throughout our 32 married years, continues to amaze me and helps me weather this storm. If she bears no anger and has no fear, how then can I when she is the one suffering this disease?

Day 30 PC

Patience

August 15, 2012

Throughout this entire journey, God is definitely teaching me greater patience. I do not suffer errors of omission ("I forgot") well, and today we encountered our second in the past few days. Originally, Mildred and I expected her to begin chemo this past Monday, August 13th, but because the oncologist's office was late scheduling her PET scan, her scan was done on Monday. We then expected her first chemo treatment today, Wednesday, August 15th. Imagine our frustration (primarily me) when we met with the oncologist, reviewed the PET scan, and found that no one from his office had scheduled the treatment for today. Our doctor thought his assistant had taken care of it, but she was waiting for a set of orders from him to do so. Needless to say, in a life-and-death struggle such as this, I was not pleased to lose more time. The earliest they can begin her treatment is this Friday. But Mildred prefers having her treatments on Monday so she has Monday evening and Tuesday (her normal days off from the salon) to recover from any side effects. Once the day of the week is established for the first treatment, then each of the subsequent treatments will be the same day of the week on an every-other-week basis. She will still need to have lab work done on the in-between Mondays, as well as return to his office each Wednesday after a Monday treatment to have the pump removed. Each of the treatments involves wearing a medical pump for 48 hours that will inject her with one of the four drugs. The end result of all this is that she is now scheduled to receive her first treatment on Monday, August 20th. In the meantime, we sit and wait to get in the battle.

Mildred and I were deeply touched last night by the members of our church life group who came to our house for dinner. We talked, shared our experiences, and prayed with them.

Then they gathered around the two of us, anointed Mildred with healing oil, laid hands on us, and lifted us up to our God in prayer. It is moments like these that we will look back on and treasure when we complete this journey. There are not enough words to adequately describe the amount of love, support, and prayer we have received from each of you. We continue to draw our strength that God is providing us through you.

> **JENNIFER**
>
> When I first went on chemo, I received four treatments. After my fourth treatment, I almost didn't make it, but my Savior brought me back. He gave me strength. He gave me peace. I was afraid because I thought the chemo had burned my esophagus. I ended up in the hospital with a severe infection of my gastrointestinal tract.
>
> My friend Jennifer, who had Stage 4 colon cancer, had recently been told her cancer had returned. She resumed chemo right before I started mine and had four treatments. She ended up in the hospital with severe complications from the chemo. Her symptoms were very similar to mine, and she did not make it. She had been hospitalized shortly before I was. That made me very fearful when I was hospitalized after my fourth treatment.

Day 34 PC

Reality and Sadness

August 19, 2012

The reality of what we are dealing with was driven home earlier today when Mildred and I learned of the death of Jennifer, a dear friend of more than 20 years who was diagnosed with the same condition as Mildred, only two months earlier. Jennifer had surgery to remove part of her colon a little over two years ago. Her one-year CT scan was clean, but her two-year scan showed the cancer had returned and advanced to her liver and lungs, much the same as Mildred. Jennifer had gone through five of the six chemo treatments with the same drugs Mildred will start receiving tomorrow. Her body's reaction to the drugs caused her to be hospitalized a little over two weeks ago with pneumonia and dehydration. It appeared that she was making slow but steady progress through Friday of this week, but everything changed on Saturday.

Jennifer was a kind-hearted person who loved the Lord and now has the privilege of residing with Him. The rest of us can only aspire to that. I ask each of you who reads this to please lift up her husband, Kevin, and their two teenage boys, Eric and Mark, in prayer as they grieve for their wife and mother. Please pray that God will give them strength as they endure this sad, difficult time.

Day 35 PC

Chemo Begins

August 20, 2012

Today was the first day of chemo, and we were both anxious and a little afraid of what would transpire. We found comfort from two individuals who were both on their last day of chemo before having surgery. They both reassured us that anything we had been told was worse than what they had gone through. While they did have some side effects, including the loss of hair for one of the ladies, their overall perspective was that it was not as bad as they thought it would be. Needless to say, this helped ease our fears.

Throughout the day, other patients who were receiving chemo stopped by and talked with us about their diagnoses and treatments. It became apparent after one day that there is definitely a camaraderie among those receiving treatment. While no one wished to be there, everyone was glad to be able to talk with someone else who knew what they were feeling and understand.

For now, Mildred does not feel any different than she did before receiving treatment. Hopefully, that will continue, although we have been told that the side effects do not really occur until after the second or third treatments. Mildred would like to attend our friend Jennifer's viewing and funeral in Raleigh, but it will depend on whether the side effects cause her any problems. We are praying they do not. We continue to lift up Kevin, Eric, and Mark as they grieve, and we ask you to do the same.

Day 36 PC

Side Effects

August 21, 2012

The day started out well as Mildred rested and ate normal foods. However, by 6:00 p.m., the side effects of chemo began. She experienced a quick onset of nausea followed by vomiting. The doctor had prescribed the anti-nausea drug Zofran, which she immediately began taking. She also began experiencing a sensation of coldness, even though her body temperature was normal. She went to bed, and I covered her with a sheet, two blankets, and a comforter to help her stay warm. She is drinking eight to 10 glasses of Gatorade, fruit juices, and water per day to remain hydrated. She tried to fall asleep, but she just could not nod off, even though she only had two hours of uninterrupted sleep last night. Finally at 8:30 p.m., she agreed to take the tranquilizer the doctor had prescribed, Ativan, to help her sleep. By 9:15 p.m., she had fallen asleep.

Day 37 PC
Side Effects Continue

August 22, 2012

At 11:30 a.m., Mildred was vomiting again and experiencing the cold sensations. I gave her another Zofran, but it did not seem to have any effect. She was scheduled to visit the oncologist at 1:30 p.m. to remove the 48-hour pump they had put on her on Monday. The oncologist's physician assistant (PA) came to the treatment room, examined, and interviewed Mildred, and then decided to infuse her with a stronger nausea, vomiting, and sleeping drug. The PA told me that Mildred would probably sleep for a few hours and that when she awoke, I should give her another Zofran and an Ativan to help her go back to sleep. If the drug works, the PA expects that Mildred will return to normal by the weekend.

On this journey so far, we take it one day at a time, are thankful for each day, and pray there will be another. Your continued prayers and support are greatly appreciated.

Day 38 PC
Side Effects Continue

August 23, 2012

Mildred awoke this morning at 6:30. Although she was tired, as opposed to sleepy, she felt better than she had the day before. She did not have the nausea and vomiting, and she was much more alert and aware than she was the night before. After I bathed and dressed her, we went to the salon to visit with the girls and clients for a little while and then to her 11:00 a.m. appointment with the oncologist. They gave her the same hour-and-a-half infusion of the drug they had given her the day before. She had taken a Zofran when she woke up and again after finishing her infusion. They want her to take this medicine through Saturday, and hopefully there will not be any reoccurrence of the vomiting. They plan to strengthen the medicine with the next chemo treatment in hopes of reducing or eliminating the vomiting. She has been able to eat cereal and two bowls of soup over the course of the day without any negative effects, so hopefully they have found the right solution.

Mildred and I were saddened that we were not able to attend our friend Jennifer's funeral today and ask that each of you continue to lift up Kevin and his two sons in prayer. We can only imagine the grief they are dealing with and hope they will find solace and peace in God's loving embrace.

We continue to take it one day at a time and hope that each day is better than the previous day. We continue to pray to our Lord for a miraculous cure, for He is the only one capable of that. We will continue to follow the medical protocols, but we understand that they are only capable of slowing this thing down. Our ultimate success totally depends on God.

Day 42 PC

Exhaustion

August 27, 2012

Over the last few days, Mildred has been completely exhausted. In our 32 years of marriage, I have never seen her so tired, even in appearance, as she has been these last few days. She has so little energy that she cannot even dress herself.

The medical staff says her exhaustion appears to be within the normal body reaction to the chemo, and she will continue this pattern throughout the remaining five chemo treatments. Each week she receives chemo, she will be exhausted for the first week, and then each day of the second week she will improve slightly until she receives the next treatment.

We continue to pray that God will give us the strength to endure this phase of our journey and that He will deliver the miracle of healing for her.

Day 46 PC
Soaking Prayer

August 31, 2012

On Saturday morning, our pastoral staff and elders are going to do a "soaking prayer" for Mildred where they all lay hands on her, anoint her with oil, and pray for her healing and recovery. We continue to be blessed by the love, support, and *prayer* we are receiving from every direction. I can only hope that our God will answer all these prayers and remove this deadly disease from Mildred's body so she can return to a normal life and continue to praise His name. If He chooses to do so, Mildred and I both agree we will spend the rest of our time sharing the miracle of her healing and glorifying His name to all.

Day 50 PC
Chemo #2

September 4, 2012

Today was Mildred's second infusion of chemo drugs. Based on the reactions she had to the first chemo, they added an anti-nausea drug to her IV to prevent a reoccurrence of vomiting. Throughout the day, she has been more like herself than at any time since we first found out she had cancer. Her vitality and her spark have been present. She was able to visit the girls at the salon after six hours of chemo, do some grocery shopping with me, and host 12 members of our church life group at the house this evening. She did not take any naps today due to her abundance of energy. I can only hope this will continue over the next two weeks and she will not experience any of the side effects she had after the first treatment.

We continue to pray for miraculous healing from our God every day, and we are so thankful for all the prayers from each of you and your individual prayer networks. There is no doubt that Mildred has an army of prayer warriors lifting her up constantly. As Mildred says each and every day, "He's [God's] got it, so I have nothing to worry about."

Day 53 PC

So Far, So Good

September 7, 2012

So far, so good. It has been three days since Mildred received her second chemo treatment, and she is doing great. She has not had any vomiting or nausea, and she hasn't been extremely tired. We spent time at the salon after her treatment, and she was able to laugh and enjoy the girls' company. Today she went out to lunch with her sister and a friend, and then they went to see a movie. We are very encouraged and pray she will not have any fatigue over the weekend.

Mildred's appetite seems to be getting better as well. Although she lost 19 pounds since Day 1 PC, she has gained 3 pounds back. It must be all that great food everyone has been bringing us. We appreciate all the prayers and support. We pray every day that our God will work a miracle in her that the world can only marvel at.

Day 63 PC
A Bump in the Road

September 17, 2012

Mildred was scheduled to receive her third chemo treatment today. Unfortunately, her white blood cell count—the cells that enable the body to fight off infection—was too low. Instead, she received an injection of Neupogen, a drug designed to raise the white blood cell count. They will continue to give her an injection of this drug each day until her labs show the white count is back where it should be. Once the labs have been normal for a week, she can resume her chemo treatments.

In the meantime, Mildred has to be extremely careful of who and what she comes in contact with. Since her white count is so low, any infection or disease she has contact with could potentially be fatal. Thus, she cannot go to the salon. And she can only eat cooked foods—nothing raw such as fruits and vegetables.

Needless to say, we were not expecting anything like this when we went to the oncologist's office this morning. At first, it was like a punch in the gut since she had not had any negative side effects since receiving the second chemo treatment. However, after a few hours passed, we came to see this for what it is—just a bump in the road. Throughout this journey, we know there will be good days and not-so-good days, and we just have to keep on marching forward. When we encounter the good days, we give thanks to our God for them, and when we encounter the not-so-good days, we ask Him to give us the strength to persevere.

That is why we chose the "Footprints" poem and logo for this website. We know there will be days when He and He alone carries us through.

Day 70 PC
The Journey Continues

September 24, 2012

Mildred had her labs on Wednesday, September 19th and again this morning. Thankfully, both lab results indicated that her white blood cell count had returned to the normal range. As a result, her third chemo treatment is now scheduled for next Monday, October 1st, assuming the count remains stable.

Mildred spent an hour or so at the salon today and is planning to spend more time there on Tuesday, Thursday, and Saturday. She is eager to have some semblance of normalcy, although she will not be able to stand behind the chair while she is having chemo treatments. But just being able to spend time with "'her girls" and interacting with the friends and clients who come to the salon will be an emotional uplift for her. We pray that her physical strength will be sufficient to enable her to have a positive impact on all she comes in contact with.

Day 77 PC

A Good Day

October 1, 2012

Today was one of the good days on this journey. Mildred had her labs this morning, and then we met with her oncologist. After reviewing her labs since the beginning of her chemo treatments, Dr. Steinberg stated that all her blood markers are trending in a positive direction. In addition, her weight has stabilized in the 145-pound range over the last few weeks. The outward signs are that we are winning the battle. The only negative thing she has begun experiencing is a slight loss of hair, but the average person would not know it. I told Mildred if her hair loss reaches a point where she wears a head bandana or a wig, I will shave my head bald to match. Oh boy, will that be a sight to see.

Mildred had her third chemo treatment today after seeing the doctor and will return on Wednesday to have the pump removed that she wears for 48 hours as part of the treatment. She will have new scans done the week of November 19th (Thanksgiving week), and we will meet with Dr. Steinberg the week of November 26th. We are expecting to receive the best possible Christmas present we have ever had during that meeting. We continue to marvel at the strength our God continues to provide us on this journey. While we understand one possible outcome of this, we simply are not overcome with fear and distress. We know that He has this. Just as He sent his Son 2,000-plus years ago to stand in our place, He is carrying us through the "mud" right now. As a dear friend related to us about the vision she saw for us, when this is over, we will shout to the world and stand before all as living examples of His power and His love.

Day 84 PC

Another Good Day

October 8, 2012

Mildred had another good day today when she visited the oncologist for her weekly labs. All her blood markers continue to trend positive, and her weight has stabilized, albeit after losing 30 pounds since this journey began.

She did have a rough weekend, though, suffering one of the side effects of her chemo—constipation. She suffered the effects of this from Tuesday morning through Friday evening when she took a suppository. The result was very much like trying to pass a kidney stone. She was in excruciating pain and had cold sweats from Friday evening through the early morning hours of Saturday. During that time, she was able to pass waste in limited quantities. At about 3:00 a.m., the pain finally began to subside, and she was able to sleep some. She slept most of the day on Saturday and had very little energy on Sunday. Today she was more her usual self.

We continue to thank all of you for your prayers and love. Hardly a day goes by that we don't see or speak with someone who says they continue to be in prayer for us. We also continue to receive food and physical assistance from all of you, and we are just so thankful. The journey we are on would be so much more difficult if it were not for the fantastic friends and loved ones we are so blessed to have.

Hopefully, someday we can reciprocate. May God continue to bless each of you.

Day 92 PC

The Journey Continues

October 16, 2012

Mildred had her fourth chemo treatment on Monday. All her blood markers continue to trend in a positive direction. Her weight has stabilized over the last few weeks with no additional loss. While her hair has thinned, she still has most of it, and it is not readily apparent that she has lost any. Her energy and spirit continue to remain high, and as of this evening, she has not experienced any side effects from the most recent treatment.

Mildred continues to be an inspiration to all who know her and see her. People remark that she does not appear sick. Her response is that she is not, that God has it, and that she is fine. While none of us can say what the result of this journey will be, most of us continue to believe we will witness God's love and miraculous healing power as we go forth. Mildred still has work to do in this life, and the events of this journey will only reinforce and strengthen her ability to share her testimonies of what God has done.

Day 97 PC

Another Bump in the Road

October 21, 2012

We knew when we started this journey that there would be good days and not-so-good days. The past few days have been of the not-so-good variety. After Mildred received her fourth chemo treatment last Monday, all was going well on Tuesday and Wednesday. However, on Thursday afternoon, she began having nausea, followed by vomiting that night and most of the day on Friday. When she experienced this after her first treatment, they added medicine to her chemo infusions, along with other medicine in a pill form that she takes for the first three days after treatment.

These medications had been working, and she had not had any reoccurrence of vomiting after the second and third treatments. However, this time they did not prevent the vomiting. In addition, the combination of the vomiting and the toxicity of the chemo drugs has produced irritation of her esophageal and upper stomach linings. She continued to have these symptoms when she awoke on Saturday morning. The oncologist's triage nurse who was on duty prescribed a liquid medicine designed to combat both the vomiting and the irritation. Despite this new medicine, Mildred continued vomiting throughout the day and evening on Saturday, and the irritation continued. She was either sleeping or awake but not alert and coherent throughout the day. When she awoke, she still had the nausea and irritation but did not vomit. The nausea and irritation have been constant, but fortunately, the vomiting has not happened today.

While we have placed our trust in God during this process and He has been able to provide the strength necessary to continue this journey, I would be less than honest if I did not acknowledge the level of fear this time. Mildred suffered various side effects in previous rounds of chemo, but the level of exhaustion and lack of alertness after this fourth treatment have produced genuine fear in both of us. I pray every day that God will continue to give us strength and work a miracle of healing that only He can do. However, I also know that His plan is not always our plan, and the ability to accept that is one of the struggles of our faith walk.

I ask all who read this to please lift us both up in prayer before our God tonight. This is one of those times on this journey where there is only one set of footprints in the sand.

Day 99 PC

A Long Day

October 23, 2012

On Monday when Mildred awoke, her condition had deteriorated from Sunday evening. I took her to her previously scheduled 11:30 a.m. labs appointment with her oncologist. All her labs came back within normal ranges, but her doctor examined her and recommended she go to the ER at Sentara Virginia Beach General Hospital. She arrived at around 12:30 p.m. They started pumping her full of fluids and antivomiting and nausea medicine. They also did additional blood and urine tests and a CT contrast scan since she had complained of pain in her lower abdomen. The pain was in the same area as the original tumor they removed in July. All these procedures took place over a 10-hour span. Around 10:30 p.m., the ER doctor, after consulting by phone with Mildred's oncologist, met with us to go over the results. While Mildred was severely fatigued by the nausea and vomiting, the consensus was that she should be able to combat that by continuing to drink plenty of fluids, particularly Gatorade, and taking the anti-nausea and vomiting medicine Zofran. They prescribed another drug, Diflucan, along with the "miracle mouthwash" the oncologist had prescribed over the weekend to help combat the irritation in her esophagus and GI tract. They said the irritation is actually a fungus, commonly referred to as thrush, that has developed due to the weakness of her immune system. The fungus is common to most people in the mucous membranes of the GI tract, but normally, our immune system keeps it from becoming active and spreading such as it did in Mildred.

The good news was the CT scan. The ER doctor feared that Mildred might have a new cancerous tumor in her colon, given the location and existence of the original tumor and the pain she was experiencing. Fortunately, the scan showed nothing physically solid and only showed some inflammation in her colon. The ER doctor believes the combination of the medicines they prescribed for the other conditions will gradually heal the inflammation. In addition, the CT scan showed that the chemo she has received so far is working and that the cancer has regressed compared to her original scans in July.

We were able to leave the hospital slightly after 11:00 p.m. and return home. Since then, Mildred has not had any reoccurrence of vomiting. The nausea does not seem to bother her as much, only when she sits up or tries to move around. The pain from the thrush and the colon inflammation will probably take a couple days to subside, now that she has begun taking the prescribed medicines. Hopefully, she will continue to make progress and will be able to continue her chemo regimen as scheduled.

All in all, despite a very long and emotionally wearing day, it was a positive result. Our fear and anxiety level were at a peak prior to receiving the results of the tests, particularly the CT scan. However, once again, our God demonstrated His ability to move mountains. We thank each of you for all your prayers, particularly in the last 36 hours. We know they helped get us through this latest bump in the road. We also know there will be more bumps as we continue this journey, but again, we know God has this and will see us through.

Day 102 PC

Uncertainty

October 26, 2012

This week has been a rough one for us. Mildred was in the hospital ER most of Monday. We came home late Monday evening. She spent the entire day Tuesday continuing to vomit and suffering the pain from the infection in her colon and the burning sensation from the fungus eating away her mucous membranes. We returned to her oncologist on Wednesday, and he proceeded to infuse her for about five hours with fluids and various medicines, attempting to get things under control. While there was some short-term relief from the symptoms after returning home, by late evening, the pain and burning sensations had returned. Fortunately, the nausea and vomiting had improved.

We returned to the oncologist again on Thursday. They infused her with fluids and various medicines for five hours. Again, there was some short-term relief, but late that night, the burning and pain symptoms returned. We are scheduled to return to the doctor in the morning. I do not know what will happen, but I will not be surprised if they hospitalize her, given the lack of progress in overcoming the symptoms. While she has suffered side effects after previous chemo treatments, none have lasted as long as this one. It breaks my heart to see her suffering and feeling so helpless. Other than attending to her physical needs and continuing to pray for her, there really is nothing any of us can do.

I ask each of you to please lift her up in prayer to our God and ask Him to end her suffering. Only He can heal her from this, but if that is not His choice, I ask Him to not allow her to lie there and continue suffering in pain.

Day 103 PC
The Battle Continues

October 27, 2012

Mildred was admitted to Princess Anne Hospital on Friday afternoon. The consensus of her oncologist and me was to admit her so they could continuously infuse her with liquids and medicine to attempt to overcome the chemo side effects. She will probably be there at least until early next week as they try to stabilize her, particularly for the vomiting, nausea, and diarrhea. Her blood counts are in range, but her electrolytes, potassium, and other levels continue to be dangerously low. She is physically exhausted from the past week.

The good news is that when I left the hospital this morning, she seemed to have improved slightly. She was more alert and coherent than yesterday but still nowhere near normal. Hopefully, she will continue to make progress in the next few days. This episode will set her chemo schedule back one or two weeks since they need to stabilize her first.

Thanks to all of you for your continued prayers and assistance. We could not have come this far without you and God helping us.

Day 106 PC

Progress

October 30, 2012

Since the doctors changed Mildred's meds, she has not had any vomiting, and her bowel movements are more normal. Her potassium is still lower than desired, and she is still weaker than normal but not as bad as she was on Friday and Saturday. We spoke with the attending physician earlier today, and he believes that if she is able to make it through this morning and afternoon without any adverse changes, she can come home this evening. She will need to rest and not attempt to exert herself physically, but our hope is that by the weekend she will return to a more normal condition. Again, we thank all of you for your prayers, love, and support. Our God provides us with the strength to continue this journey through the efforts of all of you.

Day 107 PC

Home at Last

October 31, 2012

Mildred was finally able to come home on Wednesday. The doctors decided to keep her overnight since she seemed very tired on Tuesday afternoon. She was stronger this morning but has slept since I got her home. The nausea, vomiting, and diarrhea appear to be under control, but she is extremely tired. Our hope is that by the weekend, after four or five days of bed rest and more normal eating, she will regain her energy level that she had a few weeks ago.

We continue to pray for God's strength to endure this journey and thank each of you for doing the same.

Day 110 PC

Rest

November 3, 2012

Since Wednesday, Mildred has been on bed rest with minimal physical movement: When she is not resting in bed, she sits in one of the recliners I moved into the bedroom for her. Her appetite remains good, although she is eating smaller portions but more frequently during the day. She remains extremely tired and weak, but thankfully no additional nausea, vomiting, or diarrhea has occurred. We continue to pray for God to give us strength in every way as we continue this journey we are on. Only He knows where we are headed, and we just have to trust Him.

Day 112 PC
Rebuilding Strength

November 5, 2012

We visited the oncologist today. Mildred's blood markers were either in normal range or above. He was concerned about her extreme reaction to the fourth chemo treatment and indicated that he has rarely seen a patient react that way. He did not have a specific cause that he could identify, particularly since there were no treatment differences between the first three treatments and the fourth. He decided not to give her the fifth treatment today but rather continue to pump her full of fluids and meds to revitalize her. She will not receive the next chemo treatment until she regains her strength, which could be a week or weeks. He does believe she will get there but is just not sure how long it will take.

His other concern is the amount of weight she has lost. Since July 17 (Day 1 PC), she has dropped 36 pounds, which represents 20 percent of her total body weight. He prescribed a new medicine that will stimulate her appetite and hopefully help her gain weight. He is hoping to see the beginning of a weight gain trend by the next visit on Monday a week from now.

The end result of the visit was that although she is still tired and weak, she should continue to progress in a positive manner. How long it will take remains to be seen, but the doctor does believe she will recover her strength and gain some weight. While the last few weeks have certainly tested our faith, we continue to trust that God has it. Your continuing support has certainly helped us continue this journey, albeit with a few bumps. We look forward to the day when we can loudly proclaim to all the miracle God has done.

Day 119 PC
One Step Forward

November 12, 2012

We visited the oncologist's office today where Mildred was scheduled to receive her fifth chemo treatment. Thankfully, all her blood markers were in range. Her blood pressure was normal, and her weight has stabilized. All in all, her lab results were very positive, considering what she has been through.

As a result, she was able to receive her fifth chemo treatment. Her doctor reduced the dosage to 80 percent of the level she had been receiving in an effort to minimize the side effects. He said he would maintain this level for the sixth treatment as well. After the sixth treatment, new PET scans will be taken, and he will then determine whether she will continue with additional chemo treatments. Hopefully, the overall effect of the six chemo treatments will be a significant reduction in the size and growth of the cancer cells.

Once again, we cannot thank each of you enough for all your prayers and support. I had the chance to speak with our missionary from India who arrived in the States last week. One of the first things he said was how much he, the staff, and the children at the school and orphanage in India I had visited and worked at earlier this year were praying for Mildred and me. I cannot begin to find the words to convey the awe and wonder we feel that there are prayers being offered for us virtually all around the world. We could never have imagined that so many people would care enough about us to continually lift us up before our God. While we do not yet know what the final destination of this journey will be, it is our sincere hope that the result of this journey will enable us to minister to those in need in ways we could not have imagined just a few years ago. If we are able to use our experiences to demonstrate God's love, we will have truly been blessed.

Day 126 PC

Mixed Blessings

November 19, 2012

After receiving her fifth chemo treatment last Monday, Mildred had a good week. She did not experience any of the previous side effects. She spent the week resting and regaining her strength, and even spent a couple hours at her salon on Friday. Earlier today, we returned to the oncologist for her weekly lab work. All her markers were in normal ranges.

In addition, her weight has stabilized over the last three weeks. She is currently scheduled to receive her sixth chemo treatment next Monday, and then sometime in early or mid-December, she will have new PET scans. They will compare them to the PET scans before her chemo treatment to determine how much progress has been made and what happens next. We know that God has this and that our journey will continue.

We have come to believe that one of God's purposes for placing us on this journey is so we can share our experiences with others and become a source of peace and comfort. God has demonstrated this to us during the treatment phase and never more so than today. Approximately six weeks ago, Mildred was asked by her nurse to speak with a young woman named Sherri in the treatment room. Sherri is a 43-year-old mother of three teenage children who was diagnosed in September with advanced Stage 4 pancreatic cancer, one of the fastest-moving cancers. On that day, she was to receive her first treatment and was very afraid. Her husband was with her but was in denial over her medical condition. We spoke with them, shared our experiences, and encouraged them. Before leaving, Sherri and Mildred exchanged phone numbers, and they later spoke by phone a couple times.

When we arrived at the doctor's office today, Sherri, along with her mother and sister from California, were in the waiting room. Unfortunately, Sherri has quickly spiraled downward and currently weighs only 76 pounds. She no longer has the strength to walk on her own and is very angry at God for causing this to happen to her. While Sherri was exposed to church as a child, she is not currently a believer. We spent time trying to help her understand that God did not cause this to happen to her and that she can find peace in this process by giving herself to God. After 30 minutes or so, Sherri and her family went to meet with her doctor, who is also Mildred's doctor, while we went to have Mildred's lab work done. After finishing the lab work, we encountered Sherri's sister and mother in the waiting room. They were in tears and distraught because the doctor told them he had to discontinue the chemo treatments and hospitalize Sherri in an attempt to make her last few weeks as comfortable as possible. We hugged both of them and cried with them.

We gave them our phone numbers and told them to please call us once they knew the details of her hospitalization so we can visit with them. We told Sherri and her family we would do anything we could. While we cannot remove the disease from her body, our hope is that we can help her renew her spirit and find peace before she leaves this world.

We ask each of you tonight to please lift Sherri and her family up in prayer to our God. Pray that she will come to know Christ in the next few days and accept Him as her Savior, even if it is with her last breath on this earth as the thief on the cross next to Christ did before he left this world. Pray that she will find eternal peace. Pray also that God will comfort and strengthen her family as they work through this time in their lives and that they, too, will come to know our Lord as their Savior. And please pray that God will give Mildred and me the words to speak to them that will bring them peace and comfort in this troubling time.

Day 127 PC

Update

November 20, 2012

Mildred had another good day without any side effects. She was able to spend a little time at the salon, and then we had the chance to visit with Sherri in the hospital. Sherri was slightly improved physically and more alert and aware. We spent an hour encouraging her to not give up and to fight the good fight. Mildred shared many of her experiences with Sherri. We prayed for her, and Mildred recited Psalm 23 and shared how much that passage has meant to her during this time. My sense was that when we prepared to leave, Sherri was not as angry but still asking, "Why me?"

We will continue to pray for her and her family and ask that each of you please continue to do so as well. We hope to visit her again over the weekend.

Day 133 PC

Optimistic Signs

November 26, 2012

Mildred visited the oncologist's office today. Her lab results were all in the normal ranges, her vital signs were all normal, and she has even gained 4 pounds in the past week. She received her sixth chemo treatment today. The doctor ordered the new PET scan for sometime next week. Once he receives the results, he will compare them to the baseline scans that were done before she began chemo treatments and then sit down with us to discuss what happens next. After the next couple weeks, we should know where we are heading. We continue to believe that God has this and that the news will be positive.

We also spent some time with Sherri today. She was released from the hospital on Saturday after receiving some IV meds and a blood transfusion. She appears more alert and aware but continues to lose weight. She still is struggling with "why me," and we continue to encourage her to keep fighting. More importantly, we continue to pray for her and ask that each of you continue to do so. We again had the chance to share what God has been doing for us on this journey and how He can do the same for her. We pray that she will seek Him out.

Day 138 PC

Crossroads

December 1, 2012

As I write this, the waiting has begun. On December 11th, Mildred is scheduled to have the new PET scan. On December 14th we will meet with her surgeon, and on December 17th we are scheduled to meet with the oncologist to review the scan and discuss what is next. Clearly, we are at a significant crossroads on our journey. We will find out what progress has been made in reducing the size and effects of the cancer in her body, and based on those results, we will make decisions concerning what treatment program(s), if any, will be next.

We continue to believe that God has this and that the news and decisions will be positive. However, even if the news is not what we would prefer, we continue to believe that God has a plan for Mildred. We will accept whatever the outcome is, trusting that our God is a loving God who has her best interests at heart. In the meantime, we will continue to pray every day for His strength and guidance. We ask that you do the same.

Day 154 PC

An Amazing Day

December 17, 2012

Our God has a tremendous sense of humor in addition to all His other qualities. Mildred and I visited her oncologist today to find out the PET scan results. The oncologist had spent the past week and a half in Israel visiting family, and today was his first day back in the office. Needless to say, his schedule was swamped, and he was running behind. We had to sit in one of the exam rooms until 3:15 p.m. while he was seeing other patients. We were not excited to be sitting in a small room staring at the walls for approximately two hours.

Our doctor came into the room, spoke briefly with us, and then stepped out so Mildred could change into the typical hospital gown. When he did that, the doorknob mechanism got stuck in the door jamb and would not open the door. For the next hour, the doctor, nurses, and staff tried to open the door to no avail. I was also trying everything from inside the room, but I did not have any tools to use. I tried paper clips, letter openers, tongue depressors, credit cards, and more, but nothing budged the mechanism caught in the door jamb. At some point, the staff contacted maintenance, which was located at a different site. A maintenance man finally arrived. He had a stepladder with him that he used to climb up and remove the ceiling panel above the door. He passed me a screwdriver, which I used to pry off the doorknob cover, unscrew the hardware, remove it from the hole in the door and then pry the stuck piece of hardware from the door jamb. Needless to say, we all laughed a lot once the episode was over. We will forever remember this day.

At that point, the doctor was able to sit and discuss with us the results of the PET scan and the comparison with the baseline scan. After the good laugh we had over the doorknob, God gave us something to cry tears of joy over. The results of the scans showed that in both the lung and the liver, the cancer nodules had either disappeared or shrunk more than 50 percent. In addition, there is no evidence of any active cancer cells, only the remnants of the cancer cells that have shrunk. Even the doctor was pleasantly surprised and said we could not have expected anything better at this point. It does not mean that Mildred no longer has cancer, but it does mean that significant progress has been made and can continue.

The plan is for Mildred to resume chemo treatments every two weeks. They will reevaluate her after the next three treatments and may do three additional treatments, depending on the circumstances. The doctor's prognosis is that three to six treatments should result in her only needing to take medicine in pill form on a regular basis and periodically have maintenance chemo.

We have truly been blessed to receive an early Christmas present from our God. We are so fortunate to receive these results and know it is the result of all the prayers each of you have offered during this journey. We can never thank you enough.

In addition to Mildred's results, Sherri is also doing better. She was well enough to attend Mildred's open house this past Saturday at the salon and has gained a few pounds. While her prognosis is still not promising, it has improved compared to what it was when we first met her. They are giving her a minimal level of chemo and are talking in terms of months, not weeks. Thank you for praying for her. We give thanks to our God.

Day 162 PC

A Most Blessed Day

December 25, 2012

As we celebrate the birth of our Lord and Savior this day, Mildred and I want to wish each of you the most joyous and blessed Christmas.

We are so blessed to be able to share today with so many of our family members, some from Oregon, New Jersey, North Carolina, and Florida.

We are so blessed that Mildred's health has progressed as shown by the most recent PET scan. We are so thankful for our network of friends who have given us such tremendous love and support on this journey. We have truly been blessed in more ways than we could ever deserve.

May each of you enjoy this special day. Take a moment to give thanks for the many blessings you have been fortunate to receive and share those blessings with someone who has not been as fortunate.

Merry Christmas!

Day 175 PC

On the Road Again

January 7, 2013

After a most blessed and joyous holiday season spent with family and friends, Mildred resumed her chemo treatments today. She had treatment 2 in phase 2 of her treatment program. She is expected to have one to four additional treatments before they take another PET scan to determine how much progress has been made. Her lab results today were all in the normal ranges. The only negative was that she has lost weight again and is currently down to 141 pounds. It sure seemed like she was eating plenty over the holiday season. It's just another bump in the road, and we continue marching forward. Thanks be to God!

Day 189 PC
Onward We Go

January 21, 2013

Mildred had her appointment with the oncologist today. All her lab work came back in the normal ranges, and she has gained 3 pounds. After reviewing her results from the first two treatments in phase 2 and all her lab work, her doctor plans for her to receive six chemo treatments in phase 2. She has already received three. That will take her to mid-March, and then they will rescan to determine how much progress has been made. He is pleased with the progress so far and that she has not had any serious side effects from the treatments since they lowered her dosage. He remains cautiously optimistic about what the next PET scan will show. We continue to believe that God is working in her and through her to a glorious conclusion.

In that regard, Sherri is also doing much better. She is receiving chemo on a weekly basis. She continues to regain some of her lost weight, although she is still significantly below normal. Her attitude is now positive, her level of faith has increased, and her prognosis continues to improve as her time lengthens. Looking at the results so far for her and Mildred, I do not know how anyone could deny the existence of our God. The two of them are living examples of what prayer can do, and we continue to thank all of you.

Day 203 PC

More Twists and Turns

February 4, 2013

The past two weeks have been another one of those periods of time when we have to adjust to some good things and some not-so-good things. Mildred had her next chemo treatment. All went well with the treatment. She should complete her phase 2 treatment in another month and then have another PET scan to determine the progress.

However, she spent most of the day this past Thursday in the hospital with stomach pains. They performed another CT scan and an ultrasound and determined that she has gallstones. The hospital sent her home with some diet changes and pain medicine, but her oncologist believes that surgery will be necessary to remove the stones and possibly even her gallbladder. He is scheduling a consult with the surgeon who performed her original surgery this past July when the cancerous portion of her colon was removed. Once we meet with him and he has a chance to discuss everything with us and the oncologist, a decision will be made. Our hope is that the surgery can be performed laparoscopically, which would involve significantly less pain and recovery time than conventional cutting and would minimize the impact on her chemo regimen. Once again, we remain in God's hands.

We thank all of you for your continued prayers and kind thoughts.

Day 217 PC

One Day at a Time

February 18, 2013

Probably the most personal lesson I have learned from this journey is to take things one day at a time. Throughout most of my adult life, I have always been a planner and organizer. I analyze the problem, devise solutions, implement the best solution, and evaluate the results. I always believed that process enabled me to control the eventual outcome of whatever I had to deal with and how I would respond to it. God has now taught me that was nothing more than an illusion. He was, is, and always will be in control of our lives. The last few weeks have powerfully brought that lesson home to me.

As you know from my previous post, Mildred's oncologist and the ER doctor believed she had gallstones and would need surgery to remove them and possibly her gallbladder. They scheduled her for a HIDA scan this past Tuesday. The scan takes about two hours. They inflate and then deflate the gallbladder while taking pictures to determine the gallbladder's ability to function properly. On Saturday prior to the test, Mildred developed an abscessed tooth that was causing severe pain. We spoke with our dentist on Monday, and he indicated there was nothing he could do for her until after the scan since he would need to anesthetize the area to perform any work. So Mildred had to suffer with the pain until Tuesday. Immediately after the scan of the gallbladder was done, we visited the dentist's office. The dentist wanted to treat her with antibiotics and pain meds first and then see her again on Friday.

On Thursday, we met with her surgeon to review the HIDA scan results. The test showed that her gallbladder was functioning normally. She does have one or more gallstones, but the doctor does not believe surgery is advisable. Given her overall condition and the fact that the stones are not causing any blockages, he advised her to modify her diet to liquid, low-fat, soft bland foods to help minimize the gallbladder's workload and to take pain meds if the pain persists. He wants to see her again in a month to confirm his initial treatment. On Friday, we went to the dentist, who pulled the abscessed tooth. The dentist continued her on the antibiotics for the corning week and pain meds as needed.

After all that, we felt we could get back on the regular routine with her fifth chemo treatment. Well, that was not going to happen. We went to the oncologist today, and they took Mildred's labs. Her platelets were too low to receive chemo. After reviewing the HIDA scan results and the surgeon's opinion, the oncologist believes the pain in her stomach area is most likely occurring in her liver. Given the level of infection in her liver from the cancer (about 90 percent), the elimination of the gallbladder as a potential cause, and the fact that she has been having numbness in her hands and feet (neuropathy), he believes it is necessary to change the chemo treatment regimen she has been on. Since the first treatment, she has been on FOLFOX. The new regimen she will be on is called FOLFIRI. While he believes this will reduce or eliminate the neuropathy, he cautioned us that the liver may not respond. He intends to stick to the original plan of six treatments in phase 2. After that, he will have another PET scan done and see where she stands.

Sitting here a few weeks ago, I could never have imagined that we would experience the events that have occurred these last few weeks. I will try to make the best of today and do the best I can for her while not giving any thought to what might happen tomorrow or the next day or thereafter. I have no clue what any future day may bring, and I can only deal with today's events.

Most importantly, I have truly learned that God is in control of this and that each day will be whatever He chooses it to be. Mildred has said from the beginning that God told her He has it. She is able to rest comfortably in His embrace. I, on the other hand, have had to struggle to accept that I have no ability to control or even influence what happens. But I have come to a point of acceptance. I have learned to accept that I can only do the best I can to help her and take care of her. The remainder of what happens will be determined by God, and I can only trust that He has a plan for her and for us.

Whatever that plan is, Father, convict our hearts and give us the strength to see it through.

Day 223 PC

Prayer

February 24, 2013

I seek out each of you this evening and humbly ask you to pray for Mildred, me, and our family. Our journey seems to have more bumps in the road lately than we have had before. This morning, Mildred's cousin Blanche, who had bone cancer and was about the same age as Mildred, passed away in Robeson County, North Carolina, where most of Mildred's family is from. She had been ill for a while, and it was not totally unexpected, but she had only been placed on hospice a couple days ago. We also found out that our sister-in-law Beverly, who has been married to Mildred's brother Johnny for almost 40 years and also is about the same age as Mildred, had a major heart attack and is in the intensive care unit of Pinehurst Memorial Hospital in North Carolina. They operated on her, placed a stint in her heart, and tried to repair some of the damage, but her heart is only functioning at approximately 50 percent.

Please lift all of us up in prayer as we are really in need of God's strength right now. Thank you.

Day 231 PC

Another Bump in the Road

March 4, 2013

We met with Mildred's oncologist today. What we expected to happen and what did happen were different. We thought she would receive her next treatment in phase 2 of her program and then have a new PET scan. However, the oncologist decided to add an additional treatment with the new regimen before having the scan. So Mildred had treatment 6 today and will have treatment 7 on Monday, March 18th, followed by a new PET scan on Monday, March 25th. We will then meet with the oncologist on Friday, March 29th to discuss the scan results and the next phase of her treatment. All in all, it's not too bad.

The other thing I want to share with you is what occurred in the treatment room today and what has been occurring more so in this phase 2 of her treatments. As we were leaving to go home after her treatment, I called her Pastor Mildred. While she may not have the formal theological training that most pastors have, she has the heart, the rock-solid level of faith, and the life experiences to effectively minister to people who are in need and going through their own rough times. She had the opportunity to meet and spend time talking with four patients she had not met before. She was able to listen to their individual stories, share her own story, and provide comfort and love to them. It just comes naturally to her. It is one of the gifts God has given her.

Every time we visit the oncologist's office, both the nursing staff and the administrative staff are always so glad to see her and love on her. One of the treatment nurses today commented on how she could feel the love from Mildred every time she is there. In addition to the patients she met today, she continues to see other patients she has come to know over the last few months. She still speaks once or twice a week with Sherri, who is continuing to improve spiritually and physically.

Mildred's positive attitude has been grounded in her faith in God throughout this process, despite the bumps in the road. She is truly an inspiration to those around her. When we reach the point in this journey where she no longer requires chemo on an every other week basis, I do not know what God has planned, but I continue to believe more and more that active, everyday ministry in some form will be part of it. I cannot imagine that God will deliver her from this sickness and not put her in a position to tell her story to others who are hurting and in need of someone to share God's love with them. She truly is one of His special angels.

Day 245 PC

So Far, So Good

March 18, 2013

Mildred visited the oncologist today. All her lab results were normal, so she received her seventh chemo treatment in phase 2. On Tuesday, March 26th she will have her scan, and on Good Friday morning, March 29th, we will meet with the oncologist to discuss the results of the scan and what will happen in phase 3.

As always, she met two new friends today and had a chance to tell them her story. She also saw five of her existing friends and was able to share the events of the past couple weeks with them and uplift them.

As we await the meeting on Good Friday, we continue to know that "He has this." We do not believe it is a coincidence that we are meeting with the oncologist on Good Friday. Surely this is another part of God's plan, and we are expecting nothing but good news, if not an outright miracle. What a blessing it will be to share both God's good news and our good news on the same weekend. We continue to be so thankful for all He has done for us on this journey, and we look forward to continuing our walk forward on this path He has placed us on.

Day 252 PC
Another Hill to Climb

March 25, 2013

Mildred received her last chemo treatment in phase 2 on Monday, March 18th. After two days of feeling "normal," she began to experience fatigue and diarrhea on Thursday, March 21st. Since she had experienced this before, she took the previously prescribed meds to combat these symptoms. Unfortunately, they did not work this time, and she got progressively worse as each day passed. By Sunday evening, March 24th, she had uncontrollable diarrhea, extreme fatigue, pain in her lower abdomen, swelling of her hands, and dehydration.

When she awoke on Monday, March 25th, she had the same symptoms and fell to her knees and passed out for five to 10 seconds. Fortunately, I was in the bathroom with her and caught her before she struck anything. I immediately took her to the Princess Anne Hospital ER. They began the usual battery of blood, urine, and stool tests, and began pumping fluids into her. Her potassium was low, her white blood count was low, and her electrolytes were completely out of whack. They also did a contrast CT scan of her lower abdomen, chest, and head. The scan showed that she had inflammation and infection in her colon and esophageal linings. They were the same symptoms and conditions she had last October when she had thrush and severe dehydration.

She was admitted to the hospital. They continued to pump fluids and antibiotics into her. The doctors have scheduled an ultrasound for tomorrow for her lower abdomen to ensure that nothing else is going on, but they seem to be fairly confident that this is a repeat of October. If so, it will probably take three to four days for her to get back to "normal," but at least this time they don't have to spend a couple days testing and diagnosing her.

While this is more than just a bump in the road, it is simply a hill to climb. We continue to believe that these events are just part of our journey and that when all is said and done, we will both emerge stronger for the experiences and be able to use them to minister to others. Our ability to say to someone else, "I understand what you are feeling" is markedly enhanced when we have previously experienced their pain and emotions. God continues to mold and shape us so we can make a difference for others.

Day 255 PC

Progress

March 28, 2013

The ultrasound they did confirmed the original diagnosis. Mildred continues to experience diarrhea and is only able to drink liquids. Over the course of the day, her fatigue level improved somewhat, and by evening she was able to converse in a relatively normal fashion. They are still pumping her full of potassium and other regenerative fluids, as well as antibiotics. It will probably be two or three days before they have the infection and inflammation under control and she is able to eat soft solid foods.

Her oncologist visited her this morning in the hospital, and while he did not go into detail about the CT scan and her next phase of treatment, he did say we would meet as scheduled, even if we had to do it in the hospital, to discuss what's next. He did say that the scan did not show any new cancer cells or growth of existing cells. Our belief is that on Friday he will tell us of reductions in existing cancer cells and discuss a less rigorous treatment schedule for phase 3. We just continue to take it one day at a time and trust in God's healing power. He still has this!

Day 256 PC
A Test of Faith

March 29, 2013

Mildred made some progress during the day on Friday. Her blood markers (white cells, potassium, etc.) were all back in the normal ranges. Her diarrhea continued to lessen, and they switched her to soft foods. She is still fatigued and battling the infection and inflammation in her esophageal and stomach linings. The GI doctors want to evaluate her on Saturday morning, but their thinking was that if she continues to show improvement, she could be discharged on Saturday afternoon and rest at home.

If only Friday evening had been as positive as the earlier part of the day. She began vomiting—four times. They gave her some additional meds, but this was the first time since she had been in the hospital that these symptoms appeared. Hopefully, she just had a reaction to eating solid foods for the first time in over a week.

But the real punch in the gut came from the oncologist. Mildred's CT scan did not show any improvement or worsening of the cancer when compared to her December scan. After the seven treatments in phase 2, there was no additional progress. He did not go into detail about what's next, preferring to let her build up her strength and recover from this series of side effects. We are to call his office once Mildred gets home.

Needless to say, Mildred received the news in better fashion than I did. She continues to rest on the fact that "He has this." I expected a more positive result. I know the true test of faith is continuing to believe when we do not receive what we prayed for. I also know that God is in control of this process and that it may not turn out the way I want. I will continue to pray every day for strength and healing, but in the end, God's will shall be done. I will accept whatever He decides.

Day 266

Home

April 8, 2013

Mildred was able to return home but continues to be extremely fatigued. She has been able to eat some solid food without having diarrhea or vomiting, and her blood markers continue to be in the normal ranges. She will keep taking a pharmacy of pills over the next few days, and hopefully that will restore her to normal. We thank all of you who have visited at the house during the past week and also those who provided meals. We covet your prayers and are offering our own since prayer is the only thing we have to lean on right now.

Day 268 PC

Mixed Results

April 10, 2013

We visited the oncologist this morning. The overall result is that some slight progress has been made. Her weight has decreased another 4 pounds; she is currently at 127 pounds. While she has not had any reoccurrence of the side effects that caused her to be hospitalized, she has had a physical heaviness in her body since leaving the hospital. She constantly feels like she is carrying concrete blocks, particularly when she attempts to move around.

The oncologist recommends another round of six chemo treatments given every other week beginning Monday, April 15th. He also believes it is necessary to reduce the dosage levels 50 percent of the original level she was receiving when she began treatment last September. Based on her body's reaction to the two prior regimens, he fears she might not survive another episode like the two that put her in the hospital in October and a couple weeks ago. The trade-off, however, is that the effectiveness of the drugs will be 50 percent of what they were at the beginning of treatment, and the rate of progress will be correspondingly slower.

The end result of everything today is that we continue to march forward, even if it is at a slower pace. As the oncologist said, "As long as the scans and lab work reflect progress, we should continue them." While we were hoping that the scan results and our meeting would eliminate the need for the chemo every other week, we take comfort that some measure of progress is being made. We will trust that our God "has this." While the speed of the journey may not be quite what we would have wanted, we believe God has a plan and that the plan will be in accordance with His will, not ours. While we will undoubtedly encounter additional bumps in the road, we *know* that God is with us. We find comfort in the words of the poem "Footprints." When there is only one set of footprints in the sand, they are His, not ours.

We have been so blessed to have such a tremendous network of friends and family around us giving us additional strength and peace. So many people have come into our lives since this journey began that we can never find the right words to convey the proper level of thanks. Our hope is that we will someday be able to minister to others as we have been ministered to during this journey.

Day 273 PC

Continuing Progress

April 15, 2013

We visited the oncologist's office today. They did the usual blood work on Mildred, and the results were all in the normal ranges. In addition, she has gained 2 pounds compared to last week's weigh-in. As a result, she was able to receive her chemo. Since she received the infusions last Wednesday, her energy and alertness have improved. She was able to spend a couple hours on Saturday at the salon and go to both her Bible study class and church service on Sunday. She has definitely made progress compared to where she was one week ago.

She also had the opportunity to meet three patients in the chemo treatment room who she had not met previously. She was able to share her story with them. One was a 37-year-old mother and nurse who also has Stage 4 colon cancer. Needless to say, Mildred was able to provide encouragement to them and testify to all God has done and is doing for us.

We thank God for your prayers, words of encouragement, food, and more. I cannot imagine how anyone could endure a journey such as the one we are on without the love and support of dear friends and faith in God. We truly have been blessed.

Day 287 PC
Another Day of Ministry

April 29, 2013

Today Mildred visited the oncologist's office to receive her second chemo infusion in phase 3 of her treatment. All her lab markers were again in the normal range, and her weight seems to have stabilized for the time being at 127 to 129 pounds. During the course of last week, her strength and energy returned to more normal levels. She was able to spend a few hours on Thursday and Saturday at the salon with the girls and clients. That is always a positive experience for everyone.

I am amazed at the ministry opportunities we have every time we visit the oncologist. We have a chance to see the people we have come to know during this journey who are also on their own journey. The camaraderie and presence of the Holy Spirit is noticeable each time we see them and discuss how they are doing and where they are on their journey.

However, the most impact-filled experiences occur when we

have the opportunity to witness and share with someone we have not met before. Today we had the opportunity to meet a middle-aged woman named Donna who was in the treatment room for the first time with breast cancer and obviously scared. She had no one with her to help calm her fears or lean on for support. As was the case with us in the beginning, fear of the unknown creates a picture of something far worse than what really occurs. We were able to share our experiences with her, and Mildred shared the love and support she has received from our Heavenly Father. She discussed the side effects she has experienced but most importantly the recovery she has made each time. She shared the strength she has received throughout this journey, which helped calm Donna's fears.

The chance to minister to others who are suffering the effects of cancer, combined with a higher level of closeness that cancer has brought between Mildred and me, have made this journey so worthwhile. While I can't say we would choose to have cancer given a choice, the fact that God placed us on this path and has given us so many opportunities to meet and help people has been so rewarding. Our experiences have enabled us to know firsthand what others are feeling and experiencing in their most fearful moments. It is our own "moments in the fire" that have made a difference for others and have brought me to a level of faith I have not had before in my life. While I have always said that Mildred had a level of faith I could only aspire to, I have come much closer to that level as a result of this journey.

Day 294 PC

Expanded Ministry

May 6, 2013

Mildred visited the oncologist today for her in-between lab work. All her blood markers were in normal ranges, and her weight continues to stabilize at 127 pounds. She had a good week after receiving her chemo last Monday. She was able to visit the salon on Saturday for a few hours and visit with several clients as well as her girls.

As I have written about previously, every time we visit the oncologist, it seems like God puts people in front of us to minister to. Today, we met a young woman in her early 30s named Carla. You could tell just by looking at her that she was the proverbial deer in the headlights. Her husband was with her, but they both were scared and upset. It was their first time in the treatment room since they were recently told she has leukemia. Mildred happened to pick the chair next to her and began a conversation. We both were able to share our experiences with them and share what God has done for us. Carla and her husband are both Christians but were still very scared and emotional. We talked about how we were at that point on our journey and how we have progressed. We shared how many times we have encountered what we now characterize as bumps in the road and that each time we have come through a little stronger and more certain of God's presence. Most importantly, we were able to reaffirm God's presence in their lives and help them focus on Him.

When we finished and got ready to leave the office, Mildred's nurse, Gay, came over and thanked us for spending time with Carla and her husband. She said how much the nursing staff appreciates when we come, how much of a difference we make in other patients' lives, and how we are able to calm their fears and help them renew or gain their faith. Gay said she wished we could be there every Monday, Wednesday, and Friday since so many patients could use our help. A conversation then ensued how to make that a reality. Mildred and I said we would be willing to come for a few hours each of those three days when Mildred would not normally be there for treatment so we could minister to others. We both feel that God has been leading us into deeper and stronger ministry and that this may be one of the ways He plans to deliver us there. We concluded the conversation by asking Gay to speak with Dr. Steinberg, Mildred's doctor and one of the founding partners of the firm, to see what his thoughts are. We would be perfectly willing to meet with him to discuss a plan on how to implement this and establish boundaries. We are hopeful that he will be willing to discuss this and that from it will come more opportunities to help others. If God intends for us to do this, He will open the door. We await His answer.

Day 301 PC

More Good News

May 13, 2013

Mildred was at the oncologist's office today for the full spectrum of services. Her weight continues to stabilize at about 127 pounds. All her lab work was within normal ranges. Everything seems to be heading in the right direction. Dr. Steinberg was encouraged enough with her progress that he decided to rescan her after four rather than six treatments in this phase. She received her third treatment today and is scheduled to receive her fourth on Tuesday, May 28th. He is scheduling her for another PET scan during the first week of June, and we are scheduled to meet with him to review the results on Monday, June 10th. We have every reason to believe that the news will be positive, both due to Dr. Steinberg's assessment and more so due to our faith in God. We just know that He has this!

We continue to be given ministry opportunities. Mildred was able to visit in the treatment room with seven patients she had met previously. Their conditions range from Stage 1 breast cancer to Stage 4 brain cancer. In each case, they were able to draw strength and encouragement from her. It is as if they all have become brothers and sisters sharing common bonds and experiences. While none of us know what their individual outcomes will be, they each are able to come away from the conversations with a stronger, more peaceful perspective.

Mildred also had an opportunity to minister to someone new. While she was getting treatment, they brought a man in on a gurney to receive treatment. He was an existing patient but was suffering the type of side effects that had required Mildred to be hospitalized—dehydration, electrolyte imbalance, semicoherence, and so on. His wife and young daughter (mid-20s) were with him, and you could see that they were petrified, not having been through this before. The daughter was crying and very afraid. Mildred got up from her treatment chair and went to speak with the wife and daughter. She assured them that he would be okay and related her own similar experiences. She shared with them her faith and was able to calm the daughter in particular. Mildred finished her treatment and left before the staff finished attending to the man.

We are also hoping that we will soon be able to begin ministering to other patients on a three-day-a-week basis. Dr. Steinberg has given his approval and is trying to arrange a discussion between us and the practice's administrator to review the parameters and address potential issues. The final decision will be up to her, and we are hopeful and praying that we receive approval. We simply believe that God has placed us there not just to be healed but to be part of the healing process for others.

Day 316 PC

Steady as She Goes

May 28, 2013

Mildred had her labs and chemo treatment today. All her labs were in the normal ranges, and her weight continues to stabilize at 126 to 130 pounds. She has not experienced any significant side effects. She is scheduled to have a new PET scan next Wednesday, June 5th, and then we meet with the doctor on Monday, June 10th. We remain optimistic that progress will be evident.

We were able to take our first trip away from home this past weekend since last September. My mother in New Jersey had to have skin cancer surgery, so Mildred, the three dogs, and I drove up to spend four days with her. Mildred enjoyed being away from our new normal and spending time with my mom. It was a nice respite. I will have to return to New Jersey this Thursday since my mother is having cosmetic surgery to repair the open wound from last week's surgery. Mildred's sister, Marie, will be staying with her while I am away until Sunday evening.

We also were able the previous Saturday evening to prepare and serve dinner to Sherri and her family. What a delight it was to see all her family so positive in their outlook. Sherri is still making progress, and we are so thankful for what God has done for her, her husband, and especially her children. We remain convinced that He has placed us on this journey to serve, and we believe He will continue to evidence progress in Mildred so others can truly see His power and glory. What an awesome God we serve, and we believe there will be more evidence of that in two weeks when we receive the PET scan results.

Day 329 PC
Disappointed but Thankful

June 10, 2013

We returned to the oncologist today to review the results of Mildred's latest scan and discuss the next phase of her treatment. We were disappointed with the results, having expected more significant progress. The scan showed there was no change in her lung, but there were reductions in the cancerous lesions present in her liver and abdomen. The tumor markers in her blood are trending downward, which is a positive result. Also, her current lab work reflects all normal range results, and her weight has improved by 3 pounds to 129 pounds. The end result is that she will continue on her current FOLFIRI regimen of receiving chemo treatments every other Monday with lab work preceding each treatment and on the in-between Mondays. While none of the results today were negative based on the physical progress she had been making since changing to the FOLFIRI regimen, we had greater expectations. Thus disappointment reigned, albeit temporarily.

God has a way, if we look and listen, of showing us that He remains in control and that everything is proceeding according to His time and His plan. Once we went to the treatment room, we were confronted with examples of this in four different instances. The first one happened in the treatment chair next to Mildred. An older couple came in to receive treatment. The wife, who was in a wheelchair, was in a very weak state, barely able to remain awake. After she began treatment and then fell asleep, we had a chance to speak with her husband, who shared with us their journey and God's presence. His wife has Stage 4 lung cancer that has metastasized to areas of her rib cage, liver, and abdomen. She is currently in the latter stages of treatment, and they do not expect her to survive more than three to six months. He shared that while he does not want to lose her, they both have accepted that God is planning to call her home, and they find comfort in their faith and pray that He will ease her suffering before she goes home.

The second instance was a couple we have known for over 10 years when we all attended Atlantic Shores Church. Clyde was in one of my Bible study classes, and Mary was in Mildred's class. We have seen them periodically since Mildred began receiving treatment because Clyde was receiving treatment for brain cancer. I had a chance to speak with Clyde today in the waiting area and found that he, too, is in the last stage of treatment, primarily for pain relief. The medical staff has told him to get his affairs in order as they only expect him to live another 30 to 60 days. While he waits for his time to come, he is very thankful for the life he has had and that he has had time to say his goodbyes to his family and friends. His only worry is the effect his passing will have on his wife, Mary.

However, he finds comfort in knowing that she will be embraced by God's love, as well as the love of family and friends, and that he will soon have the opportunity to meet God face to face.

The third instance was a patient, Anthony, who was diagnosed with Stage 4 colon cancer and began treatment the same time as Mildred. Anthony is approximately 40 years old. The doctors just told him there is nothing more they can do for him and that his only chance of survival is to enter a clinical trial program at Duke University. Absent any successful new medicine, he is not expected to survive more than 60 days. We have spoken frequently with Anthony during the treatment phase and have repeatedly shared our faith with him. Before today, he always seemed more of a party guy, but today he seemed to have genuine interest in what we had to say. He said he would remain in touch with us by phone and hopefully be able to see us and learn more about what faith has done for us on this journey.

The final instance was a slightly older woman who entered the treatment room and sat next to Mildred on her other side. Upon striking up a conversation with her, we found that she was diagnosed with Stage 2 breast cancer in 1994 and then with Stage 4 bone cancer in 1999. She shared with us how she went through chemo treatments similar to Mildred's for a few years before reaching a point where she was able to take chemo in pill form and come in to be examined and treated once every few months. She said she leads a normal life and that she and her husband travel frequently, visit with their children and grandchildren, and just enjoy living. While she knows cancer will always be present in her body, she firmly believes it will not get any worse than it currently is.

After returning home, Mildred and I discussed the day's events. We both agreed that it was as if God sent four different messengers to us to enable us to gain perspective. Who are we to be disappointed in what He has done? We are achieving progress at whatever pace He decides. After listening to each of the four individuals, we cannot help but be encouraged about where we are and continue to believe that He has placed us on this path for a reason. We will continue to praise and glorify Him on this journey and be thankful for all He has enabled us to do.

Day 343 PC
Continued Progress

June 24, 2013

Mildred visited the oncologist's office today. All in all, it was another blessed day. All her lab work is in the normal range, and her weight has remained steady in the 125 to 130 pound range. She received her second chemo treatment in phase 4. She has seemed to be rejuvenated in the last four weeks, more so than at any other time since being diagnosed. She has repeatedly stated that she feels like she used to feel prior to being diagnosed. She is spending more time in the salon and plans to be there four days a week for four or five hours each day. Although she is not yet ready to resume her duties, she is becoming more active in the business affairs of the salon on a daily basis and loves seeing everyone. She also delights in getting to see many of the friends she has made during her treatment times.

Today she probably had six conversations with other patients she has met, not to mention the various staff people who adore her. One of her friends, Joyce, said today how Mildred simply glows when she is in the treatment room. She just has a presence about her that uplifts everyone around her. Many have come to not only admire her but grow in their own faith walk. We stopped by the salon today after treatment and had a conversation with a woman who used to work for Mildred. She was there with her husband, and they both remarked how inspiring Mildred's journey has been to them and how much of a difference reading the CaringBridge updates has made in their lives. They were once nonbelievers but have come to know the Lord by following our journey and testimonies. It is just another example of how you do ministry every day and often plant a seed with someone you never met or knew, and then it bears fruit.

One request we would like to make tonight is for each of you who reads this to please pray for Clyde and Mary. We saw them at the treatment room today, and Clyde continues to worsen. When we last saw them, the doctor said, "any day." Clyde is receiving pain medication, and Mary said he sleeps three-quarters of the day. She does not expect it to be much longer. We spoke with Clyde, and he is definitely ready to go home. He just wants it to be over, and he no longer has the will to live. We pray that God will take him peacefully and that Mary will find comfort. We also pray that she will find sufficient strength from God's presence in their lives. May God bless both of them and each of you.

Day 365 PC

An Entire Year

July 16, 2013

Today is the one-year anniversary of Mildred's diagnosis and life-changing event. We give thanks to God that He has accompanied us on this amazing journey that has changed our lives so greatly. When we look back at all that has taken place this past year, we rejoice in the many blessings God has bestowed on us. We have met so many new people who have become part of our lives. We have had the opportunity to minister to and share our blessings with many others. We are making progress against the cancer, and each successive PET or CT scan is showing progress compared to the previous ones. The depth and magnitude of our faith in God has grown so much—exponentially for me. It truly seems as though we have begun a new life, much as someone does when they go from being a nonbeliever to a believer.

As we begin our second year, we simply pray that God will continue to give us ministry opportunities to reach those in need of His love and mercy. We have been so blessed as we have been led to share those blessings with others. We hope that these updates will somehow touch you and lead you to do likewise.

Day 371 PC

Much to Be Thankful For

July 22, 2013

Mildred had her next chemo treatment today and continues to make progress. All her labs remain in normal ranges, but her weight has declined to 124 pounds. Her tumor markers are moving in the right direction, and she has repeatedly stated that in the last six to eight weeks she has been feeling the best she has since before being diagnosed over a year ago.

We remain so thankful to God for all He is doing in our

lives. Mildred's health is improving, and we continue to have the opportunity to minister to those we meet. Whether it is in the treatment room, Mildred's salon, our life group, or elsewhere, we are given opportunities to share our story with others and hopefully invigorate them with God's love. We seek your prayers for patients such as Clyde, Anthony, Sherri, and others we have met and who are walking on their own paths. We particularly covet your prayers for Clyde and Anthony who may be in the latter stages of their personal journeys. May our God comfort them and their families and, if it be His will, heal them from all sickness and disease.

Day 385 PC

More Thanks

August 5, 2013

Mildred had her next labs and chemo today. Once again, all her labs are tracking positive, remaining in the normal ranges. Her tumor markers still show progress, and she has not had any serious side effects of the chemo since her regimen was last changed. Most importantly, she has gained 5 pounds since last week. She was weighed on two different scales to ensure an accurate reading, and both indicated she had gained 5 pounds. We are so thankful that our Lord heard the prayers for her to gain weight.

Today's session included meeting with her doctor, who basically said to just keep doing what she is doing since it appears to be working. He is thinking her next scan will be sometime in mid-September. Until then, she will receive chemo every two weeks and take the appetite stimulant the doctor prescribed.

We also spoke with Sherri, who is doing fine as well. We continue to lift up Clyde and Anthony and their families in our prayers and ask that you do likewise. We also want to ask that prayers be given for Leonard, an older gentleman we met in the treatment room. The last three weeks he has been unable to receive treatment because his white blood count continues to decline. It has been very frustrating for him and his wife, and they feel so powerless. Leonard has been weakened to the point of needing a wheelchair, and we simply ask that you ask God to give him strength and elevate his white count so he can receive treatment again. Most importantly, we ask God to let them know He is with them, despite the temporary setback, and is embracing them with His love.

We thank each of you for your love and support.

Day 400 PC

Keep Marching

August 20, 2013

Mildred had her next chemo treatment and labs on Monday. Again, her labs were all normal, and her tumor markers had decreased in size. Her weight was up 3 pounds. Other than occasional fatigue and diarrhea, she has not experienced any side effects normally associated with her chemo. We continue to give thanks for the progress she is making and pray it will continue. She will have her next scan sometime in mid to late September. Hopefully, it will reflect progress.

We keep marching on and give thanks and praise for all the blessings God has bestowed on us during this time. We eagerly await a clear revelation of where and how God wants to use us and these experiences we have had. In the meantime, we are ministering to other patients and their families we come in contact within the chemo treatment room.

Day 415 PC

A Momentary Pause

September 4, 2013

Mildred had her next chemo treatment and met with her oncologist today. The good news is that her appetite and weight continue to increase. Over the last six weeks, her weight has increased 10 pounds. However, her cancer markers have plateaued. Since her regimen was changed back in the spring, she has not experienced any debilitating side effects, but the strength of the drugs was diminished. Therefore, her markers are not showing significant improvement or significant regress. The doctor plans to give her another treatment on Monday, September 16th and then follow up with another scan sometime the week of September 23rd.

We will meet with him on Monday, September 30th to discuss the scan results and the next phase of her treatment. Assuming the scan confirms what the markers show, we will be between the proverbial rock and a hard place. If we increase the strength of the drugs, we run the risk of significant side effects again. If we do not increase the strength, she will most likely remain at the current plateau or begin to decline.

As we have said throughout this process, we are on a journey without a clear end in sight but with God's footprints alongside our own. It is easy to be true to your faith when everything is headed in a positive direction. However, it is a time such as this when the true mettle of your faith is tested and shaped. We have reached a fork in the road with two choices. We do not yet know which one to choose and will wait on God's wisdom to reveal itself. Perhaps He will lead us down an entirely different path than either of the ones we currently contemplate. Maybe it will be a path we could never in our wildest imaginations have thought of. We can only wait and trust that He will continue to "have this." We do know that He has brought us this far for a purpose, and we eagerly await what He will reveal to us.

Day 427 PC

A Day of Remembrance

September 16, 2013

Mildred had her chemo treatment and labs today. Her labs were all in the normal ranges, and she also gained another pound, weighing in now at 132 pounds. She is scheduled to have her PET scan on Wednesday, September 25th, and we will then meet with the oncologist on the following Wednesday, October 2nd, to discuss what is next. It is all in God's hands.

We experienced sadness over the weekend when we found out that Clyde, one of the gentlemen we had asked you to pray for, was called home last week. He was a devoted Christian, husband, and father. He was married to his wife, Mary, for 49 years. When I think of Clyde, the word *commitment* comes to mind, not only in describing him but also in describing Mary. She attended to him throughout their journey and was always there for him. Please lift Mary and their family up in prayer this evening. Pray that God will give her strength and peace as she begins a new journey on her own. Pray that the love she experienced with Clyde will remain in her heart for the rest of her days until she, too is called home where they will meet again.

Day 436 PC

Be Still

September 25, 2013

The past week has not been the best for Mildred. She had a chemo treatment last week and for the first time in a long time really suffered the side effects. Over the weekend she had severe diarrhea, nausea, and fatigue. As she started to turn the corner on Sunday evening, she began having back pains, which has since escalated. She is scheduled to see our family doctor tomorrow afternoon.

Earlier today, she visited the oncologist's office for her weekly labs. Unfortunately, she has dropped 3 pounds, her platelets and red count are below normal, and her blood pressure is up. The decision was made to let her see her family doctor regarding her back pain before treating these symptoms. The thinking is that they may all be related to a common cause. After leaving the oncologist's office, Mildred went across the street and had her PET scan.

During the past week, my anxiety level was initially high as I observed Mildred's physical symptoms. Not knowing what is causing the back pain and watching her experience the side effects resulted in a high level of uncertainty and fear on my part. However, our God always seems to know what we need and when we need it. Mildred and I were blessed both Monday and Tuesday evenings by various members of our life group who prayed over us, laid hands on us, and anointed us with oil. We truly felt the presence of the Lord in the room, which had such a calming effect on us.

Then during the day today, it was as if God Himself spoke to me. Out of nowhere and without reading my Bible, my head and heart were filled with a scripture verse from the Psalms—"Be still and know that I am God." It was the scripture equivalent of the vision and words that Mildred experienced earlier on this journey—"I've got this."

Why do we allow the human emotions of fear and anxiety to overtake us when we have the Holy Spirit and the presence of the Lord with us? We simply need to focus on Him. He has had a plan for us since this journey began, and He will guide us all the way through it. Waiting has never been a strength of mine, but I know this: *Be still for He is truly God.*

Day 438 PC

Update

September 27, 2013

Mildred went to our family doctor's office yesterday for her back pain. The timing was fortuitous since she had just had her PET scan on Wednesday, so the doctor was able to access the scan. It did not show any bone or structural damage, so his diagnosis was that somehow she had pulled a muscle in her lower back. They put her on muscle relaxers and anti-inflammatories, which made her sleep a great deal. The doctor could not tell her anything concerning the cancer, stating that it would not be proper since it is our oncologist's place to discuss that. So we wait until next Wednesday to meet with Dr. Steinberg and determine the next phase of treatment. "Be still and know that I am God."

Day 443 PC
A Bittersweet Day

October 2, 2013

We met with the oncologist today to review Mildred's PET scan and discuss the next phase of her treatment. We were extremely blessed to find out that the results indicate *no new cancer cells* and *no growth* in the existing cells. While there is minimal shrinkage of existing cells, our oncologist does not expect any significant changes. He will continue the current treatment regimen for another three months and then rescan her in January. If the PET scan at that point is consistent with the most recent scan, he will change her to a maintenance chemo regimen consisting of a pill form of chemo drugs accompanied by probably a monthly infusion. As long as she is able to remain on a maintenance program, the cancer will remain in its current state, but she will be able to live a more normal life.

We also had a discussion with the doctor about Mildred's back pain. The family doctor's diagnosis of a pulled muscle was clearly in error. The PET scan results clearly showed that she has a mild compression fracture of the L1 vertebra. The oncologist is ordering an MRI so they can have a clearer picture of what is happening, but his feeling is that the chemo, combined with the preliminary onset of osteoporosis, has caused her bones to be more brittle than normal. She will be more at risk now for mild strains, pain, and fractures, but effective pain management will allow her to heal from this incident. She will just have to be careful going forward not to physically strain herself or it could happen again.

We are so thankful for what amounts to a very positive report and results. As most of you know, my anxiety level was higher than normal going into this meeting. I was particularly fearful that the cancer was growing again as evidenced by her hair beginning to grow again. My thinking was that the chemo, which is designed to kill fast-growing cells, was no longer effective. If her hair, which has fast-growing cells, was growing back, so was her cancer. However, the doctor explained that the hair loss caused by chemo occurs when it is first administered. The initial shock of the chemo drugs kills off the hair cells, but they then develop almost an immunity to the chemo and return.

Mildred is currently receiving chemo treatments and will receive additional treatments through January. All her lab results were normal today. In addition, she has gained 8 pounds in the last week. Her weight was 137 pounds. I don't think we could have been any more blessed than we have been by these results. We give God all the praise and glory, and we thank Him for walking alongside us on this journey.

However, as is typical of this entire journey, we also received another bump in the road. We found out that Sherri, the young mother we have been ministering to since early on our journey, took a turn for the worse. She suffered two seizures this past Friday, and one of them occurred in the oncologist's office. They took her across the street to Princess Anne Hospital and then transported her to Norfolk General Hospital. The doctors determined that she has two inoperable cancerous masses in her brain that caused her to have intercranial bleeding and ultimately the seizures. Right now we ask that each of you lift Sherri and her family up in prayer. We pray that our Lord will wrap her and her family in His loving embrace and bring them peace.

We had the chance to visit with Sherri this afternoon. She is home resting. They have given her meds to manage the pain. They have been able to temporarily stop the bleeding in her brain, but the prognosis is not good. They do not advise surgery given her condition and the high degree of risk with this type of surgery. She is scheduled to meet with the oncologist in two weeks and discuss what her options are. In the meantime, she can only stay home, rest, and manage the pain. She described her pain when we were with her as more like a normal headache as opposed to the intense throbbing she experienced over the last few days.

At this point, Sherri is truly in God's hands. If He intends to work a miracle, He will. If not, we just ask that everyone lift Sherri and her family up in prayer for strength, healing, and peace. There but for the grace of God go we.

Day 455 PC

Prayers

October 14, 2013

I write this posting with a tear in my eye and a heavy heart—not because of anything with Mildred but because of Sherri. We were told today that the oncologist told Sherri there is nothing more they can do for her to defeat the cancer. The two masses in her brain are inoperable and growing. While pain medicine can be used to reduce the pain, the oncologist has recommended that hospice be contacted. Her prognosis is, at best, three to six months. Her oldest daughter is 17 weeks pregnant, and Sherri hopes to be able to see her first grandchild. We can only pray that God will surround Sherri with love and peace and give her body the strength to be able to see her first grandchild enter this world.

At times like this, I struggle to understand why God does what He does sometimes. I know people die from cancer every day, but when someone young and still full of life is taken, it is difficult to come to terms with it. As a young boy at the age of nine, I watched my father be diagnosed with MS and over the next four years go from a healthy young man of 30 years old to a bed-ridden invalid who could not control most of his bodily functions before he died. I have always had difficulty in my relationship with God over this. I would rather see myself or even Mildred be taken home as opposed to a young person who still has so much more to live for. I can only pray that God will not let Sherri and her family suffer any longer than necessary and allow her to see her new grandchild.

We ask that each of you please pray for Sherri and her family and ask God for His mercy.

Day 466 PC

Surgery

October 25, 2013

Mildred had an MRI last week to more accurately determine the extent of the compression fracture that was causing her back pain. During the past three weeks, she has been in severe pain in her back, and the pain medicine was of minimal value. The MRI determined that she has a compression fracture of the LI and T12 vertebrae in her back. The radiologist said she could let nature take its course and eventually it would heal, but the question without an answer was how long that would take and could she handle the pain during that time period. The alternative would be to have surgery where they would inject concrete in its liquid form into her back where the fractures were located. After the concrete hardened, it would act as a support for the two vertebrae and eliminate the pain. The chances of success for this procedure were estimated at 85 to 90 percent. Mildred made the decision to have the surgery.

As a result, we were at Leigh Memorial Hospital at 7:00 a.m. this morning. The procedure took approximately one hour, and by 10:30 a.m., she was in a recovery room. After resting and letting the sedation wear off, she was able to come home at 1:30 p.m. She spent the afternoon resting in the recliner and periodically sleeping. The doctor said it would take 24 hours for the pain to begin to decrease.

On Monday, she will receive her next full chemo treatment, and we will visit with her oncologist to discuss her progress. In the meantime, I ask everyone to please pray for Sherri and her family.

They began hospice treatment for her this past Tuesday, and she is experiencing severe pain despite being medicated. We continue to pray that God will grant her the mercy and the ability to make it to the birth of her first grandchild.

Day 468 PC

Update

October 27, 2013

While my initial observations were that the pain Mildred was experiencing should be eliminated by the surgery, Saturday proved otherwise. She awoke Saturday and Sunday mornings with the same level of pain she had prior to the surgery. I spoke with her nurse who spoke with her oncologist. He prescribed a stronger pain medicine to get her through the weekend until we meet with him in his office on Monday when she is scheduled for her next chemo treatment. We will discuss other possible sources of the pain and treatment procedures. We continue to pray that God will remove the pain from her and allow us to continue to move forward on this journey. We also thank each of you who continue to lift her up in prayer.

Day 469 PC

Broken Hearts

October 28, 2013

I don't know how to find the right words in a time such as this. Our friend and fellow journey traveler, Sherri, left this world this evening at 5:30 p.m. No one expected the end to come so soon. Mildred and I are trying to find God's peace in knowing that she did not lie there and suffer and that she had accepted Christ as her Savior and now resides in His heavenly kingdom. However, our humanity suffers the pain and grief of losing someone who had become so dear to both of us. We feel also for her family—her husband, George, who has lost his adult-life companion; her children who have lost their mother and soon-to-be grandmother; Sherri's mother, Maureen, who was with her during the last few weeks; and all her siblings. We pray for all of them that God will give them some measure of peace and comfort as they process this time of grief and loss.

I also pray that He will give Mildred and me strength—strength to be able to serve George and Sherri's family in whatever way they need us. We also need strength to deal with the obvious thoughts of there but for the grace of God go we. None of us know when our time will come, and surely Mildred and I know we may not have much time of our own. However, we have said from the beginning that "He has this," and it is in that statement that we find refuge and comfort. We *do* know that no matter what happens, the two of us will be together for eternity in God's kingdom. Any earthly separation will only be temporary.

We ask each of you to pray tonight for George and Sherri's family. Pray that our God will give them strength and peace as they remember their loving wife and mother.

SHERRI'S MOM, MAUREEN

Sherri met Mildred in November 2012 at their oncologist's office. Sherri was 43 years old and very sick with pancreatic cancer. She was very slender and looked older than her age. Mildred organized a prayer group for Sherri and visited her in the hospital on Thanksgiving Day. They formed a friendship that continued until Sherri died.

Mildred and Bob brought many meals to Sherri's home to feed her husband and children. Mildred was always encouraging and lifting all of them up. She surrounded Sherri and her family with love and prayer. Before Sherri died, Mildred was able to lead her to faith in our Lord. Accepting Christ as her Savior made Sherri's last days lighter. She and Mildred became like sisters, part of the same family. Mildred and Bob were always available, always there, friends 'til the end.

Day 480 PC
A Memorial Service

November 8, 2013

This evening we had the privilege of attending the memorial service for our friend and fellow traveler, Sherri. Mildred was asked to speak as part of the service. Despite having suffered excruciating back pain for the last few weeks, it was as if the good Lord touched her body and removed the pain. When she took the pulpit and spoke, you could see that she was born to be there. Her ability to speak before an audience of over 100 people and reach them through sharing her own experiences and those she and Sherri shared was amazing. Her passion and her calmness, her physical demeanor and spiritual presence connected with those who heard her. The service was indeed a blessing to Sherri's family and friends as we celebrated her life and, more so, her newfound life with Christ.

After the service, there was a reception. I have attended many events where I watched politicians work the crowd, but tonight I saw the Holy Spirit move through the crowd in the form of Mildred. Although she had never met the vast majority of those who attended, Mildred moved from one person to another with ease and expanded on her testimony with each one. None of it was preplanned. Her ability to connect with the people was truly amazing to watch. In the course of the conversations, she met another woman who is also a Stage 4 colon cancer patient and has survived for 11 years. I am convinced more and more that God has many more of these opportunities yet to come for us. Often people think of ministry as the pastor's or church's responsibility, but God has called each of us to minister in some way.

We saw the oncologist this past week, and he is thinking that Mildred's increasing back pain is disc- or nerve-related. He doubled her pain medicine. On Monday, she will have her regular chemo treatment. On Tuesday she will have MRIs taken of her upper and lower back. On Wednesday, she will have a bone scan. Once the results are sent to her oncologist, we will meet with him to discuss the next step.

As I look back on these past 16 months, I am in such awe and amazement at all God has brought about in our lives. Everything I have written on this CaringBridge site does not begin to adequately explain the many things He has done. While many see these events as trials and tribulations, we have come to embrace them as manifestations of His presence in our lives. He is molding and shaping us. He enables us to be a blessing for people like Sherri and her family. How many more Sherris are out there that we have yet to reach?

SHERRI

When I first started my chemo, I met a gentleman named Anthony who was sitting next to me. We started to talk and found out we both had Stage 4 colon cancer. As the day went on, I met several other people. We introduced ourselves, and as the weeks went by, we became friends. One day when we were all getting our chemo, I told one of the ladies, Ruth, about the card with the horse on it. A lady in the corner had her Bible out, and everybody was listening to me talk about the card and the horse. I felt like we were doing a Bible study. One person looked up, and we all started to laugh because we were all hooked up getting chemo.

The next time I went to get chemo, Anthony and I were talking about how we had both just been in the hospital recently. While we were discussing our hospital stay, a young lady joined in our conversation. Her name was Sherri. As I got ready to leave the treatment room, I hugged Sherri's neck and left. A few minutes later, my nurse came running down the hall crying, hugged my neck, and told me I had no idea what I had done for that young lady. It was true; I did not know that I had done anything, but they thought I had.

The following week I had to go back to the office for lab work. My husband came with me. We were sitting in the waiting area where a lady was talking about her sister and how bad of shape she was in. Finally, she opened her phone and showed us her sister. Her sister was Sherri. I asked this lady if Sherri was there, and she said yes, that she was here to get her lab work. When Sherri came out to the waiting area, her skin was black, very black because she was so sick. She had pancreatic cancer. She went to the treatment room ahead of me. When I got there, I went to where Sherri was with her mother and sister.

When her doctor, also Dr. Steinberg, came in, he told them that Sherri could not have any more chemo. He told them that she only had three more weeks to live. He sent her across the street to Princess Anne Hospital. However, the Lord put her heavy on my heart. I went to bed that night thinking about and praying for Sherri, and I woke up the next morning thinking about and praying for her. I asked my husband if he would take me to the hospital to see her. When we arrived, she looked so much better. They had given her blood transfusions to make her feel better. While I was there, I read Psalm 23 to her. I told her that she and I were in the shadow of death right now. I told her that I was going to march as hard as I could, and if she wanted to march with me, we would march together.

We kept in touch. We talked on the phone. However, something kept telling me that I needed to meet her children. When I had a good weekend where I did not have chemo, I made dinner for Sherri and her family, and my husband and I took it to their house. Sherri, her husband, her two children, my husband, and I were able to sit down and break bread together. After meeting her children, I felt like the Holy Spirit was telling me I was supposed to meet her children so they could see me as a person who had cancer and was doing okay. They could then accept the fact that their mother had cancer.

Those children had not had a chance to digest the fact that their mother had cancer. It had all happened so fast. The night turned out to be a great night, and they thought I was a good cook. After that night, Sherri and I roamed together. We hung out together and talked on the phone almost daily.

She became like a little sister to me, and I tried to look out for her.

You never know who God is going to put in your path. Every time I go to the oncologist's office, I always meet someone. I always feel that the Lord puts them there, and then I have the opportunity to minister to them and let them know what He has done for me on my journey. Sherri died on October 28, 2013. I had met her in October 2012, and she died a year later. I was dealing with my back, so I did not think I would be able to go to her funeral, but my Heavenly Father told me I should go. At the funeral, Sherri's mother and husband wanted me to sit with the family because they were grateful for all I had done for Sherri. A strange thing happened while I was there. Something told me to go up to the podium to speak. It wasn't me speaking; it was the Holy Spirit speaking. I was able to tell everyone about Sherri and who she was. Afterward, it was amazing to me to have kids and adults come up to me and tell me what a good job I had done. I also met someone that night who had been dealing with cancer for 11 years. It was amazing that this all happened through Sherri. I still keep in touch with Sherri's mom, her husband, and children.

Day 499 PC
Another Bump in the Road

November 27, 2013

On Tuesday, November 26th, Mildred had a second surgical procedure to relieve the pain in her lower back. After the first procedure was performed, another compression fracture of the next lower vertebra was found. The same procedure, simply one vertebra lower, was performed. Post-surgery, the doctor indicated that the procedure went normally and everything was where it should be. However, while Mildred was still in the recovery room, she began to experience significant pain. She was unable to elevate in the bed without severe pain.

Later in the day, her pain began to decrease, so the doctors decided to let Mildred go home. Her pain, which was 10 yesterday on a scale of 1 to 10, had moderated to a 6. She would rest at home and take pain meds for the next few days. That would provide sufficient time to determine whether the pain is post-op surgical pain or due to something else. If it is post-op, the doctors believe she will be pain-free by the weekend. If she still has pain at that point, she will need to see her oncologist. She is already scheduled to be there on Monday. A treatment plan that deals with the chemo's effect on her bones and the possibility of osteoporosis will need to be developed.

We are so thankful that the pain at least has moderated to a tolerable level. Mildred will not be very mobile the next few days, but hopefully by the weekend she will be more normal. We still have much to be thankful for, particularly when we consider all that has transpired over the last 16 months. We are blessed in so many ways.

Mildred and I wish each of you a joyous Thanksgiving and ask God to bless each of you and that you in turn will bless others. We all have much to be thankful for this special day.

Day 524 PC

The Journey Continues

December 22, 2013

This past month has been the most difficult part of this journey. After having had two surgeries on the compression fractures in her back, Mildred is no better off than before they were done. She continues to be in pain—some days a 3 and other days a 6 or 7 on a pain scale of 1 to 10. She is on a 24-hour-seven-day-a-week pain patch that she wears. She spends her days sitting in a recliner. She also sleeps in the recliner at night because the pain level increases significantly when she attempts to move to or from a vertical position to a horizontal position.

Given the surgical results or lack thereof and the various tests and MRIs, our oncologist thinks the source of the pain is most likely nerve- or disc-related, with disc-related being more likely. The MRIs did show some mild inflammation in two of the discs in the source area of her pain, but given the fractures that were revealed, everyone at the time felt they were the most likely source of the pain. It is now apparent that while they may have contributed to the pain, they were not the sole source of it. We are scheduled to see an orthopedic surgeon on Friday, January 3rd in the hope that he will be able to determine the cause of the pain and devise a solution.

However, as our oncologist told us, it is possible that given her age, her cancer, and her overall medical status, they may determine that surgery is too risky and instead implement a pain-management approach for the remainder of her life. If that is the case, we will have some difficult decisions to make since her quality of life has been virtually non-existent this past month, and neither of us can imagine her spending the remainder of her life in that state. I do not know if she can endure the physical and emotional suffering, and I am also not sure I can continue to watch her suffer with no solution in sight.

As far as her cancer is concerned, she continues to make progress. Her lab results show the cancer is not growing and, in some cases, is shrinking minimally. She received her biweekly chemo treatment this past Monday. However, she has suffered the usual side effects of fatigue and diarrhea since Thursday. Our oncologist continues to look toward a January new scan with the expectation that she can begin maintenance chemo as long as the scan is as good or better than the one in October. We will see what happens.

With all the above, this Christmas season is the first time in our 35 years together that we have not put up a Christmas tree or Christmas decorations. Neither of us has been able to embrace the Christmas spirit and have struggled to focus on the true meaning of Christmas—the birth of our Savior. Not only have we had to deal with all the above, but we have had to manage Mildred's salon, take care of the house, and more. And this past Wednesday, I lost someone very special to me. Sam was a business partner, a friend, and a mentor. He was one of the wealthiest people I have ever known but yet lived a simple lifestyle. His family has owned thousands of acres of land in the Williamsburg, James City, and New Kent County area of Virginia stretching back at least to the

1800s. As wealthy as he was, he lived almost his entire adult life in a simple farmhouse where he and his wife raised their family of three children. During the past 60 years, there were very few business, civic, or political events in that area that Sam did not take part in, usually in a leadership role. He was one of the most astute businessmen I have ever had the privilege of knowing. He delighted in going to Hardee's each morning for a biscuit and coffee. He gave millions of dollars and untold hours of time to charitable, educational, and spiritual causes.

His faith was as simple as he was. While he had read his Bible through and through, he was not a biblical scholar. He was not a Christian who used words to demonstrate his faith, but rather his actions spoke for themselves. He was married to the love of his life for 58 years until her death a few years ago. When Nettie was sick during the latter stages of her life, Sam became a caregiver. When Mildred was diagnosed with cancer, the first words out of Sam's mouth whenever I spoke with him were, "How's Mildred doing?" He asked me that even after he was diagnosed with cancer this past spring. Sam lived a life in his 88 years that most of us only aspire to live, myself included. I was blessed to know him and will forever remember him until we meet again.

Day 531 PC

Another Bump

December 29, 2013

The past week has been difficult. Aside from the inability to embrace the Christmas spirit, Mildred has suffered extreme side effects from her most recent chemo. The fatigue, nausea, and diarrhea have been severe, and her blood pressure has climbed to 174/112, so she was hospitalized on Friday. The medicine she has been taking to combat the diarrhea has had little effect, resulting in severe dehydration. They ran blood, stool, and urine tests to ensure that she did not have an infection. All the tests came back negative for infections but clearly showed her system (electrolytes, potassium, etc.) to be severely weakened. As a result, they gave her injections and intravenously pumped her full of fluids to restore her system. Thankfully, by Saturday evening she had recovered enough to be able to come home.

However, I had to take her back to the hospital the next morning to receive another injection and have another comprehensive blood test. She is presently resting at home. She is scheduled to see her oncologist and receive her next round of chemo tomorrow morning. Her weight has dropped again to 121 pounds, but thankfully her blood pressure has dropped to 144/79. Fortunately, the level of pain in her back has subsided to a 1 or 2 on a scale of 1 to 10, most likely due to the meds she has received in the last couple days. We are thankful for any blessing we receive.

I ask each of you to lift her up in prayer that God will not allow her to continue to suffer. I believe He has a plan for us and a reason for placing us on this path, but I am finding it increasingly difficult to see her suffer. The faith I have has enabled me to come this far, but I would be lying if I did not admit that I have been shaken. While Mildred's faith is certainly stronger than mine, it, too, has become battle-weary. Please pray that God will strengthen us both.

Day 539 PC
The Journey Continues

January 6, 2014

This past week had the usual assortment of challenges. While Mildred was able to overcome the previous week of nausea, fatigue, and diarrhea, this week had its own issues. Her back pain increased again, despite resting and continuing to wear the pain patch. We met with the orthopedic surgeon on Friday afternoon. His diagnosis was that she most likely has one or more new fractures as a result of the osteoporosis brought on by the chemo and her age. He flatly said he would not do any new surgeries. While one or more of her discs have a slight inflammation, he said the pictures of her back look better than most women he sees at her age, particularly considering she has cancer. His recommendation was to have an epidural and see if that reduces or eliminates the pain. While he did not see any downside to it, he also said it is probably a 50/50 proposition.

This morning we met with Mildred's oncologist. We discussed the orthopedic surgeon's findings and the events of this past week. His conclusion was to go ahead and schedule the epidural with one of the local anesthesiologists he deals with and also schedule her next PET scan. Once he has the results of both, we will then meet again in about two to three weeks to discuss what happens next, both in regard to her cancer and her back pain.

While we wait to see what is next, we thank so many of you for your kind words. We also thank you for the food and meals you have provided, for the flowers and small gifts you have sent, and for the many other ways you are demonstrating your love. We cannot imagine coming this far without your love and support and the presence of our Lord. You and God have truly been carrying both of us these past few months, the most difficult part of this journey. A friend of ours made the observation to us by email earlier today that our ministry in this process continues to become more powerful and reach more people because the level of spiritual warfare against us continues to increase. The more difficulty and obstacles you face, the more you know that you are effectively doing the work of the Lord. We find comfort in these words and look forward to carrying on the battle.

Day 567 PC

What a Day!

February 3, 2014

Don't ever tell me that God does not perform miracles! As I write this post, tears of joy are flowing uncontrollably. Today we had the privilege and blessing of being truly part of one of God's miracles. As most of you know, the past few months have been unquestionably the darkest part of our journey. Not only has Mildred suffered from the side effects of the cancer treatment with extreme constipation and then diarrhea, but also with extreme and debilitating back pain. She has been virtually unable to do anything except sit or sleep in a recliner or go to the hospital or doctor's office. We have not been able to attend church during this time. In addition, I began to become disconnected from God as I struggled with why He was allowing someone as special as Mildred to suffer so much. If anyone should suffer like that, it should be me. Throughout all of this, she has never weakened in her faith. She continues to trust Him, even as I began to wonder.

Despite two surgeries and a visit with an orthopedic surgeon, she has had no relief from her back pain. However, two weeks ago, on the advice of our oncologist, we went to see a pain management specialist. He reviewed her MRI and scans and discussed the compression fractures with us. He indicated that an epidural would be the best chance of reducing the pain from both the fractures and the inflammation. He administered her a high-dose steroid epidural. Over the last two weeks, her back pain is virtually gone. While she has some stiffness from sitting for a while, she says her pain level on a scale of 0 to 10 is 0 to 1. She has been able to walk without the walker. She felt so much better that yesterday we were able to attend church service for the first time in the last few months. What a joy and a blessing that was.

Today we met with Dr. Steinberg, our oncologist, to review the results of her most recent PET scan. Truly God was in the room with us because *it is all gone*! There is *"no evidence of any cancer, anywhere"* (the doctor's words). While he cautioned us that it is still possible there may be some small cells, but if they exist, they are so small that they cannot be detected by current technology. We broke into tears in the room, and tears of joy have not stopped since. Truly God has taken us through the darkest valley and never left us. Once again, the "Footprints" words say it all. He never left us, even when I began to question and wonder. God has picked us up and carried us these last few months. Words are not sufficient to thank Him.

Even Dr. Steinberg said that while modern medicine certainly played a part in this, he is not God. He has seen numerous patients with Stage 4 cancer over the years, and very few ever reach this point. In order to ensure that any small cells that may have escaped detection are eliminated, Dr. Steinberg placed her on a reduced chemo regimen. He has eliminated the most powerful and side-effect-inducing drugs from her regimen completely. He is going to keep her on the remaining drugs for the next three months at two-week intervals. Assuming nothing reappears, he then plans to change to a once-a-month treatment schedule and gradually reduce the frequency of treatments until it is a once or twice a year schedule.

When I look back at the last 18 months and where we are today, I am incredulous. While we hit various bumps in the road and went through the darkest valley, we have been blessed beyond understanding. Mildred was given two years to live when we were told of her diagnosis, and now here we are today. I think of Sherri who succumbed to this disease. I think of Sam, my friend and mentor, who also lost his battle with cancer. Why were they taken and not Mildred? Only God has the answer, but I do know this—He has a plan for us. This has not happened by chance. We now have a responsibility to share our good news with all who are willing to listen. l am not sure yet what this ministry will look like, but I know there are many other cancer patients, survivors, and caregivers who need to hear that cancer is not a death sentence. They need to hear that there is real hope and ultimately eternal life with God. As we go forward from this day, please pray for us that God will continue to lead us on this journey and that we now can become part of sharing His love with others in need.

May all the glory and thanks be given to God!

CANCER-FREE

In February 2014, after my most recent PET scan, I was told there were no active cancer cells in my body. *What an amazing day!* All my friends at the oncologist's office, the nurses, and the doctors were so happy. Dr. Steinberg, my oncologist, commented, "You don't get to see many of these." He knew how bad my cancer was, and my surgeon, Dr. Boustany, had previously told my husband to "get her affairs in order." My friend Anthony, on the other hand, could not take the chemo anymore due to the severe side effects. His doctor sent him to Johns Hopkins to be enrolled in a clinical trial. I don't know what happened to him after that, but I do know they only gave him six months to live when he left.

In the meantime, I met a "young" woman named Miss Ruth. She was a spiffy 65-year-old who was getting chemo as well. You know how it is when you meet someone who is really spiffy, when you can laugh and have a good time. That was Miss Ruth. We lost her in December 2014. I also met a woman named Linda and her husband. Linda was a walking miracle, and so was her husband. She had cancer and many other issues. Her husband also had cancer, and he was also a walking miracle 15 years later. Everyone told them he would not live. During one of Linda's illnesses, she got pneumonia, and we lost her in September 2014.

> **BACK PAIN**
>
> I started having back pain in the summer of 2013. It turned out that I had compression fractures in some of my vertebrae. I had two surgeries (kyphoplasty) to correct the fractures, but the pain continued. The orthopedic surgeon told my husband that there was nothing else he could do for my back. I went to a pain management specialist to get injections in my back to relieve the pain. The pain was excruciating and constant. I don't think I could have lived with it much longer. One Friday I was sitting in my recliner at home and on a high dose of pain medication. It was then that I got in God's face and told Him that if He could take the cancer away, then He could take the pain away, and I expected Him to do that. The next morning, I got up and realized I did not have any back pain. God had healed my back. I get stiffness at times due to weather changes, but He healed me, and I am still on the journey.

Day 714 PC

The True Test

June 30, 2014

It has been almost five months since I last posted an update. During that time, while we have encountered a few bumps in the road such as two bouts with pneumonia and a bulging disc causing irritation and pain in Mildred's left leg and groin area, we have truly been blessed. Mildred has had relatively good health, her weight has remained steady, and her scans have been cancer-free. She has been able to spend time each week in the salon and has even begun serving clients in the last couple weeks.

Most importantly, we have begun our new ministry, Voices of Hope, designed to serve the spiritual, emotional, and physical needs of cancer patients and their caregivers. We have delivered our testimony to our church and other churches that were praying regularly for us. We have continued to serve other cancer patients we have met in the treatment room where Mildred receives her chemo. We have also had a cancer patient referred to us for assistance by one of the other oncology practices in the area. Our testimony was the subject of a magazine article recently published in the *Hope* cancer magazine that is distributed to various medical facilities and cancer patients in our area. We plan to begin biweekly meetings in September for a new support group for patients and caregivers.

As you can see, God has truly blessed us and enabled us to begin making a difference in other patients' lives. During this time, we may have become comfortable and lost sight of the personal battle we are in. Not having to experience the difficult effects of the cancer treatment process we experienced in the first year and a half, we may have misplaced our battle-tested edge. Today, we were reminded that the battle is far from over. Mildred's PET scan taken last week shows a cancerous nodule in her right upper lung and another one in her right lower lung. Both nodules measure about 6 centimeters, which is smaller than most of the cancer nodules were when we began this journey but still large enough to require treatment. As a result, our oncologist has put her back on the chemo treatment she was receiving prior to February of this year. He expects that this regimen will gradually reduce the size of the nodules as it did before, but Mildred will still have side effects.

The other piece of news the PET scan showed was a new spot in the right frontal lobe of her brain. The scan could not determine if this spot was cancerous, but it definitely was not present in previous scans. As a result, Mildred is scheduled to undergo a contrast/no contrast MRI tomorrow morning, and then we will meet with the oncologist on Wednesday to discuss the findings.

After the initial punch-in-the-gut feeling for both of us, we have had time to digest and process all this information. Our conclusion is that He had it on July 17, 2012, when we were first told of her cancer; He has had it since then; He had it yesterday; He has it today; and He will have it tomorrow and thereafter. While the news today was not what we expected, we continue to believe in Him. No matter what happens, we will continue to seek and accept His will. We continue to believe that the purpose of this journey is so we can effectively minister to other cancer patients and nonbelievers as He has called us to do. The more battles and bumps in the road we are able to deal with and overcome, the more powerful Mildred's testimony becomes. We will absolutely not be swayed from this purpose. We ask that you pray for us and those we encounter. Pray that God will give us strength, compassion, and love. We thank each of you for all your prayers.

TIM

My sister-in-law Mary is an oncology nurse at a different practice than my doctor's. She recommended a gentleman, Tim, to me and asked me to contact him. I called him, and he cried the whole time we were on the phone. The chemo made him sick, and he did not want to take it anymore. His wife left him after he was diagnosed. It was so sad to hear him cry. I encouraged him to make one goal for each day and try to accomplish just that one goal. I started to talk to him about God. Tim also had neuropathy (numbness of his hands and feet), and the medications he was on made him sleepy. He could not do or accomplish anything. After approximately six months of my talking with him, he was able to talk to me without crying. He eventually started making little plans, and one night he told me he just finished putting his kitchen back together. So I told him that was a good thing and that he could make another goal for himself the next day. I never met Tim face to face, but I talked with him for approximately three years before he passed away. I am at peace knowing that he was able to go on a cross-country trip with his friend before he passed away. I wish I could have met him in person.

Day 716 PC

God's Continued Blessings

July 2, 2014

We just returned from meeting with our oncologist. Once again, God is blessing us. While the nodules in Mildred's right lung are cancerous and will require continued chemo treatment, the contrast/no contrast MRI results showed no evidence of any acute intracranial process and no evidence of any brain metastasis. Her brain is clear. The likelihood is that it was simply a cloudy image on that portion of her MRI.

She will continue on the every two-week chemo program. The doctor is confident that over time, the nodules in her lung will be eradicated by the chemo, just as they were previously. All in all, we are extremely thankful and blessed. While we have to overcome another bump in the road, we keep going on our journey with you and God walking alongside us. Oh what blessings we have received.

Day 756 PC

A New Battle Begins

August 11, 2014

Since the reappearance of cancerous nodules in her lung, Mildred has been receiving chemo every other week. She had two treatments with no side effects, but the treatment she received on Monday, August 4th made up for the first two. On August 6th, she began experiencing nausea and vomiting. For the next four days through Sunday evening, she ran the gamut of constipation followed by diarrhea, all accompanied by extreme fatigue. She slept more than she was awake those four days.

On Monday, August 11th (today), she had a regularly scheduled appointment with the oncologist. After reviewing her labs and examining her, he decided to give her fluids to build her system back up. After an hour and a half of fluids, there was no improvement. In addition, Mildred began to complain of severe chest pains.

The consensus was to immediately take her across the street to the emergency room at Princess Anne Hospital. The hospital took her right away and began examining her. Her EKG was normal, but the pain continued to increase in her chest and upper back. They did various tests and scans looking for heart enzymes, which were negative. Evidence of a pulmonary embolism was also negative. They then tested for blood clots, and the results were elevated. They did a contrast CT scan that revealed the presence of multiple blood clots in both her lungs. They followed this with an ultrasound of her legs and also found multiple blood clots there.

The attending physician met with us and reviewed everything. He put her on various meds and fluids for the next day or two to build her system back up. Assuming all goes well and no bleeding or blockages occur, she will begin taking daily blood thinners for the rest of her life. She has been admitted to the hospital and will probably be there for two to three days. We will then meet with the oncologist to discuss possible changes in her chemo regimen so no drugs are in conflict.

While Mildred is in pain for the moment, the good news is that the chest pains enabled the doctors to find and treat the blood clots before anything worse happened. The fact that she was already at the doctor's office when the pain began and could be immediately treated across the street is just another example of how our God has this. The outcome of this could have been significantly different, but everything was in place to provide for her. God continues to show His presence on our journey. While we now have a new medical situation to deal with, we remain convinced that He is leading us on this journey for a definite purpose. We will continue to wage war against what comes against us. Every day we will march onward, and *we will prevail*. Please keep us in your prayers.

Day 758 PC

She's Home

August 13, 2014

After Mildred had an echocardiogram that did not show any clots, she was able to come home this afternoon. The doctor thinks it will take about one week for her to regain her strength. We will need to return to our oncologist next week and discuss the future treatment plan. Apparently, cancer chemo patients are more predisposed to blood clots, and it is not uncommon to have to treat them. Overall, the prognosis is a positive one, and we will continue to march forward.

In the meantime, Mildred will remain on recliner rest. We are being blessed that her sister and brother-in-law are flying in from Portland, Oregon, as I write this. They will arrive Thursday morning and stay for a week to help care for her. That way she will not be left alone at any time, even when I have to run errands or go to the salon. We have also been blessed by our church family, not only with prayers but hospital visits and meals. Some of our church family visited us at home this evening and brought dinner. We also continue to be blessed by our dear friends such as the one who cut the grass today on a half-acre building site I still own so I would not have to worry about it. Our God's love is shining all around us, and we are *so blessed*. Thanks to each of you, and thanks to our God.

Day 762 PC

Another Awesome Display of His Healing Powers

August 17, 2014

Mildred and I continually give thanks to our God for all He is doing in our lives. When Mildred came home from the hospital on Wednesday, the doctor said it would probably take a week of rest and relaxation for her to regain her strength and for the pain to dissipate. Well, that may have been his schedule, but it was not our God's. Mildred improved each day, the pain was gone by Saturday, and her energy levels had returned to normal. She felt so good that she wanted to go to the salon on Saturday, but her sister and I both felt it was premature to do so. By Sunday morning, it was as if she had never had the blood clots and accompanying pain and fatigue.

We went to our church service and were so blessed by the presence of the Holy Spirit. What an incredible outpouring of His love took place in the service as we saw so many people bless us and show God's love to us and others. Mildred ate a full meal at IHOP after the service. Her appetite is as good as ever. She will remain on the daily blood thinners for the next three weeks before being rescanned to see the status of the clots. Tomorrow, we return to the oncologist's office for her scheduled chemo and lab work.

While we marvel at the wondrous power of our God, we are not shocked or surprised. We have witnessed firsthand how great He is and how He chooses to do miracles of healing. Any time we have hit the bumps in the road, He has been right next to us, giving us strength to endure and demonstrating His love for us. We have been so blessed, and we look forward to the rest of this journey. May we continue to be a reflection of His love.

A LOOK BACK

My friend Sharon made a pact with me that she would bring me dinner every week. She did that for over a year until they moved away. I remember her bringing dinner one Thursday, and I told her that all my clothes had gotten too big for me. The following Thursday, she returned with several outfits she had bought for me. She would not let me pay for them because she said she wanted to do that for me. She was, and still is, a good friend. I love her.

My friends from Bible study, Lou, and Lorraine, also brought meals over. My life group has made meals for me, and so has my sister-in-law. My sister Marie has made meals and bought me clothes. She has been by my side since this journey started. I have been blessed to have a lot of good friends on this journey.

My husband has been my rock. He has been there every step of the way. In three years, he has only missed three medical appointments, procedures, or hospitalizations. With all the doctors' appointments, hospital appointments, and many medicines, it has not been easy. But he says, "It's okay because when we made our vows, it was in sickness and in health. It was always and forever."

My sister Marie has been a huge help to me. Whatever she can do, she will do. Whether it is cleaning my house, taking care of me, or sitting with me when I come home from the hospital, she has been there. Besides Marie, my other sister Mary, who is actually my sister-in-law, has also helped along the way. The good Lord has put so many people in my path on this journey, including all the wonderful doctors and nurses who take care of me. It has simply been amazing!

I have learned many things on this journey. Before I was diagnosed, I never thought I would get cancer. How dare I put myself above anyone else. Cancer does not discriminate. In the chemo room, people get chemo weekly, every two weeks, every three weeks, and so on. You get to meet so many wonderful people. Whenever you are in the chemo room, the nurses are there to do everything they can to help you. They want to love on you, they want to help you, and they want to comfort you in every way possible. Every professional I have met since I started my journey says they love their job. For some it is even a calling, not a job. The people in those treatment rooms are very special people. When we go into the treatment room, each and every one of us are seeking the same thing. We are looking for a healer. Some of the people I have had the pleasure to meet did not seem to know how to ask for healing, but when they were called home, they knew.

This is not a journey I would have chosen for myself, but it has been an amazing journey because of all the people I have had the honor to meet. As time has passed, it has become even more amazing because of all the things and miracles God has done for me personally and all the things He has shown me. A couple times when I had a bad day, He would show me something to remind me of the day I was on the operating table—the day He told me, "I've got this, Mildred." Some of the ways He has shown me things have been so amazing.

Day 799 PC

Another Bump Overcome

September 23, 2014

Mildred was admitted to Princess Anne Hospital yesterday afternoon. She had been fatigued throughout the weekend and worsened Monday morning. We already had an appointment on Monday at 2:30 p.m. with our oncologist. After they took her vitals and examined her, they recommended she immediately be taken to the ER. Her blood pressure was 190/110, she had a fever 2 degrees above her normal temperature, she had lost 5 pounds since Thursday (now at 115 pounds), she was semi-coherent, she was coughing up mucous, and she had a rectal blood discharge.

After running various blood tests, X-rays, CT scans, and more, they diagnosed her with pneumonia and a gastrointestinal infection. Over the last 24 hours, they intravenously administered various antibiotics and fluids, which have improved her condition. Her breathing and awareness have improved. She has not had another blood discharge, but there is still some blood in her stool. They are going to do a preliminary GI exam tomorrow to see if there is anything obvious. Assuming her bleeding and blood counts remain stable and nothing is found that would require immediate attention, they will focus on getting her well and home. Sometime in the next two weeks, she will need a more thorough GI exam under sedation so they can determine the cause of the bleeding and how to repair it.

Overall, her prognosis is good, and they hope she will be able to come home either Thursday or Friday. Once again, we thank our God for seeing us through another bump in the road. He continues to provide strength and healing to us. Regardless of how many more bumps we encounter, we will not be deterred from our journey and our purpose. We continue to reach out to those we encounter—even the nursing staff today—and share Mildred's story. More importantly, people continue to witness firsthand her faith and resolve. She truly is one of God's special angels.

Day 800 PC

Update

September 24, 2014

Mildred's pneumonia improved today. While she still has some cough and congestion, her breathing is more normal, and she is not as fatigued. Assuming no adverse changes occur, the doctor plans to reduce the number of antibiotics she is receiving from four to one. Her vital signs (blood pressure, temperature, pulse, oxygen) have returned to more normal levels, and her weight is stable at 115 pounds.

The gastrointestinal doctors examined her today, and their consensus was that whatever is occurring is "serious enough" (their words) to warrant an immediate procedure rather than waiting a week or two. While the bleeding could still be the result of a fissure (tear), they believe it is more likely something else. As a result, they plan to do a complete scope of her upper and lower GI tracts tomorrow afternoon in the hospital. She will have to be sedated during the procedure, and they expect it to take two to three hours. Depending on what they find, they may be able to repair it during the procedure, but it is also possible that it will require a second procedure.

As we have found throughout this journey, different events occur that give us perspective on our own experiences. Monday morning, a 28-year family friend of one of our friends died from cancer. Earlier today, a neighbor and friend of another one of our friends passed away from cancer. Why did God choose them and not Mildred? I cannot answer that question because I certainly am not God. However, the more we encounter events such as these, the more we know that He has set a plan for us to minister to others and share our story. Even today, two hospital workers—neither one assigned to care for Mildred—stopped in her room at different times to talk with her. They had heard other staff discussing her spirit, and they wanted to meet and talk with her to find out more. I cannot explain these events in any worldly manner. I can only point to the heavens and continue to say, *"He's got this! He has had this from the beginning, He has it now, and He will continue to have it going forward."*

I ask that you lift up in prayer the families of the two individuals who passed away and ask God to bring them peace, love, and comfort. I pray also that all goes well tomorrow with Mildred's procedure, and I ask each of you to pray as well.

Day 802 PC

Home Sweet Home

September 26, 2014

All in all, Mildred had a couple good days. She had the lower and upper gastrointestinal procedure, which did not show any polyps, cancerous cells, or additional damage. She was able to come home this afternoon. She is doing much better. Her breathing is more normal, her strength has increased, and she is fussing at me again. All in all, she is back to her normal self. She will be resting at home over the weekend, and visitors and guests are certainly welcome. The doctors anticipate continued improvement. Once again, we have gotten over another bump in the road with the help of the Lord and the prayers and support of all of you. Thanks to each of you, and may God bless you as He continues to bless us.

Day 827 PC

Another Bump in the Road

October 21, 2014

One of the many things this journey has taught us is that no matter how good things may be at any point, there will always be more bumps in the road. Our faith cannot grow and expand without them. While Mildred has improved since she came home from the hospital after having pneumonia, one of the issues she has dealt with in the last six to eight months is her eyes and her sight. She has experienced almost running water at times in the form of tears. In addition, before being diagnosed with cancer, she could see relatively normal at a distance but required glasses to read anything up close. In recent months, her sight has changed to the opposite of what it used to be. Things at a distance are very blurred, and she is able to read when a book or paper is close to her eyes.

We had an appointment scheduled with our ophthalmologist the same day Mildred was diagnosed with blood clots and admitted to the hospital, so we had to cancel it. Today we were able to see him. After a thorough examination and tests, he concluded that at the moment, Mildred is legally blind with 20/400 vision. She was born with a birth defect that always rendered her left eye virtually useless, and now it is beyond anything medicine can do for it other than a possible transplant. Her right eye has developed a serious cataract that has impaired her vision. The doctor feels the situation requires surgery ASAP before it gets any worse. Mildred is scheduled to have outpatient surgery next Thursday, October 30th. He believes there is a reasonable chance the surgery will restore her sight in her right eye to normal. However, he did caution that there is some degree of risk that the surgery might not work and her vision could worsen. He also determined that her tear ducts have closed up, causing any tears in her eyes to temporarily impair her vision and run down her cheeks. He believes he can correct at least the right tear duct during the surgery and is hopeful he will be able to do likewise with the left.

I am reminded again of our "Footprints" poem. There have certainly been times when there were three sets of footprints in the sand as we walked with our Heavenly Father. However, there have also been times when there was only one or two sets of footprints when our Father carried one or both of us. This is one of those times. I know our Father will not leave us or forsake us, but I pray that He will give me strength so I can continue to walk with Him and provide for Mildred. I would not be honest if I did not admit to being tired right now. These last few months have brought new challenges as we battle existing ones. I seek His presence, His strength, and His wisdom. I covet each one of your prayers that God will provide these same qualities to Mildred and to me.

Day 836 PC

Successful Surgery

October 30, 2014

Mildred had her cataract surgery early this morning. According to her ophthalmologist, the surgery went extremely well. He did not encounter any difficulties removing the cataract and installing a new lens. He stated that her vision should be 20/30 when the eye heals, maybe even 20/20. She is home resting for the rest of today and has a patch and shield covering her eye. I have to take her for a follow-up exam tomorrow morning when the patch will be removed. The doctor would like Mildred to rest and take it easy over the weekend before resuming normal functions on Monday. She is also scheduled to receive her next chemo treatment on Monday, so we continue marching on.

I would like to take this opportunity to ask all who read this to please pray for Ann and Buz. We have known Buz for over 30 years, and during the last seven years, Ann and Buz have been traveling their own journey as Ann has battled ovarian cancer. Like us, they have had their share of bumps in the road, but they have always maintained a positive spirit and belief. Even as Ann endured the experiences of a clinical drug trial regimen, they sought God's love and strength. In many ways, they have been a role model for Mildred and me. This past week, they made the decision that the time had come to let Ann's earthly journey end naturally and begin a new one in our Father's eternal kingdom. Ann has begun hospice care and now awaits our God's final call. Please pray that God will bring them both peace and embrace them with His love.

Day 837 PC

Update

October 31, 2014

Mildred visited the ophthalmologist earlier today. He removed the patch and shield, examined her eye, treated it with more eyedrop medicine, and then tested her vision. The difference between her previous level of sight and her new level is astounding. She is now able to see much more clearly. Her vision tested out at 20/30. She is amazed how clear and lighter everything looks. She will continue with follow-up visits for the next four weeks and use the eyedrop medicines. Once again, we have been extremely blessed at the restorative and healing powers of our God. What joy!

Day 885 PC
Christmas Comes Early

December 18, 2014

Christmas came early today. We met with Mildred's oncologist this morning to discuss the latest PET and CT scans and her overall progress. Once again, we have been blessed in a way that so few are.

I had typed these first two sentences and then received a phone call from the son of a lady, Miss Ruth, we came to know in chemo treatment over the past year. She had been battling Stage 4 cancer since we met her. She was like your grandmother—small in physical stature but strong in spirit. She passed away last night. Our hearts and prayers go out to her family, and we will join them in remembering her at her service this Saturday. We lift our hands in praise that she has been called home by our Father and is free of pain and suffering.

Mildred's scans show no new cancer and no active cancer anywhere in her body. We have received the ultimate blessing on this earth. Any cancer she may have is too small to be detected by existing technology or has been eradicated. She will continue her existing chemo regimen for the next three months and then have new scans. If those scans show the same or better results, the oncologist will begin lengthening the interval between treatments. Instead of two weeks, she will go to three or four weeks, depending on the scans.

As I look back over this past calendar year, one thing has become very evident to me. When we received the news in February that the cancer was gone, we saw it as a tremendous miracle of God, which it was. However, I think that as a result of that miracle, we became complacent. We allowed ourselves to believe that the cancer was gone and would not return. Obviously, that was not the case. What we have learned is that even though God does miracles, it does not mean we no longer have to engage in battle. It's just the opposite. It is like when we first are saved. Being saved does not mean we no longer have to do battle against sin and our own weaknesses. It does mean that we now have a loving God on our side in that battle. Just as we will battle sin each and every day of our lives, Mildred and I will also battle cancer each and every day. We will keep receiving chemo treatments to prevent the cancer from returning. We will walk each and every day with our God right beside us as He has throughout this journey. We will continue to pray for, reach out to, and support in any way we can families such as Miss Ruth's who are also engaged in the battle.

Most of all, we will give praise and thanks to our God who blesses us in so many ways. We have much to be thankful for this Christmas. What an *awesome God we serve*! Mildred and I hope and pray that each of you will have a blessed Christmas and a Happy New Year.

Day 919 PC

Just Another Bump

January 21, 2015

Mildred had outpatient surgery this morning to repair the anal fissures and surrounding inflamed tissues that have been causing her pain and discomfort. The surgery went well and was performed by the same surgeon who did her original colon surgery on the first day of our journey. Mildred will have surgical pain and discomfort for two to three days as the area heals, but after that, she should be fine. Her surgeon marvels at her progress, calling her a "living miracle."

We won't let the bumps in the road limit our progress. One thing we have noticed lately is how many new people we are encountering in the treatment room and how many people have passed on that we knew previously. I attended a service a couple weeks ago for Linda, a patient we once met and ministered to. When these events occur, it really drives home to us how blessed we are. While we pray for the families who have suffered a loss, we also give thanks each day for the blessings God regularly bestows on us.

Day 957 PC

He Still Has This!

March 1, 2015

Mildred was admitted to Princess Anne Hospital on Saturday after being taken to the ER. She was her normal self on Friday, but during the night, she awoke to nausea, vomiting, and diarrhea. The symptoms persisted into the morning, and she also had pain in her arms and legs. She then began running a fever of 101 or higher.

We went to the ER where they began working on her immediately. They did X-rays, blood work, flu tests, and chest-abdomen-pelvis CT scans. After reviewing all the tests, the ER doctor and the hospital attending doctor met with me to explain the results. They believe she has a viral infection. Her body's immune system is in a weakened state from the events of the last two years. They are going to treat her with antibiotics for the infection and other meds to restore the electrolytes and combat the dehydration. The doctors expressed concern for her body's ability to fight this off and even asked if she had a DNR (do not resuscitate).

The CT scan showed that the cancer has not only returned but is spreading quickly throughout her lungs and liver. The doctors plan to consult with our oncologist in the next 24 hours and discuss their findings. They believe the immediate focus is to combat the viral infection but recommend that we meet with our oncologist ASAP to discuss our options. We hope to do this in the coming week, assuming she is released from the hospital.

I had a chance to discuss everything with Mildred. We talked for probably an hour. Needless to say, at first, we were both emotionally distraught. Certainly, this was not the result we were expecting. Her scan in late November did not show any new cancer, and the nodules that had reappeared in her lungs were gone. Our oncologist had even discussed increasing the interval between chemo treatments. Clearly it will now be a different treatment plan.

After discussing all the medical information, we had a discussion with our Heavenly Father. When all is said and done, we believe *this will be our finest hour.* God still has this. He has walked with us step by step, and He will continue to do so. Does that mean we are guaranteed another miracle? No, but it does not mean we are not. What it does mean is that we will continue to embrace our faith and rest in His loving arms, no matter what the outcome. This is the largest cancer obstacle we have encountered. What would it say about us and our faith if we allowed this event to shake us? No, that will not happen. Our Father has had this up to now, currently has this, and will continue to have it. We will not run from it.

Rather, we will embrace this as an even greater opportunity to do ministry and display for all to see His love. Fear not! He still has this!

Day 960 PC

Peace

March 3, 2015

Mildred came home from the hospital earlier today. She will be on oral antibiotics and steroids for the next 10 days to ensure the infection is completely gone from her body. She is tired but certainly much better than she was on Saturday.

We are scheduled to meet with the oncologist tomorrow morning after Mildred has her regular lab work to discuss possible treatment options. We are both calm and at peace. There is no fear, no worry. We are truly at a place of "a peace that passes all understanding." Our Father has wrapped us in His loving embrace, and we know that no matter what, it will be okay.

Day 961 PC

A Plan

March 4, 2015

We met with the oncologist for almost an hour earlier today. We reviewed Mildred's entire treatment history and scans. From August 2012 through February 2013, she was on the FOLFOX regimen, which produced significant progress but also severe side effects. From February 2013 to February 2014, we changed to the FOLFIRI regimen that produced less severe side effects as well as a clear scan. As a result of the clear scan, her dosage levels were reduced 50 percent, and the drug that gives the most side effects in the FOLFIRI regimen was eliminated.

In June 2014, her scan showed two cancer nodules had returned to her lungs. That led to restoring the irinotecan drug to her chemo and the 100 percent dosage levels. In December 2014, the FOLFIRI regimen again produced a clear scan. In January of this year, she had surgery and deferred a treatment and successive treatments for one week. Her treatments last month (February) included the chemo drug Avastin that has been part of both the FOLFOX and the FOLFIRI regimens. The question then becomes if the removal of Avastin and the skipping of a treatment in the last three months allowed the cancer to grow as fast as it has. The answer is we do not know.

After the three of us discussed all this history and how Mildred was feeling right now, we came to a decision. She will receive the complete FOLFIRI regimen with the irinotecan and Avastin drugs. She is receiving the first treatment as I write this. Her next treatment will be in 12 days, and her third treatment will be two weeks after that. Within two to three days of her third treatment, a new PET scan will be done, and we will meet with Dr. Lee, our other oncologist, on Friday of that week. We will review the scan and her response to these treatments, including any side effects. Based on that information, one of three options will be chosen. One: continue the FOLFIRI. Two: change to the FOLFOX, recognizing the more severe side effects. Three: attempt to find a clinical drug trial that is suitable for her cancer and history.

When we discussed her schedule and set the dates, I did not look at a calendar. When I arrived home and did so, I was stunned. The Friday we were scheduled to meet with Dr. Lee to review the scan and make decisions is Good Friday, leading into Easter weekend. That cannot be a coincidence. I know this is all part of God's plan.

I have complete faith that God will use this to display His love and power. Now more than ever, I am committing to Him that I will pray regularly throughout the day for Mildred's healing. I am getting out of the boat because *I know He has this*.

Day 991 PC

A Difficult Week

April 3, 2015

This past Monday, March 30th, Mildred was scheduled to receive her third chemo treatment prior to having another PET scan. When they took her labs, a significant number of measurable items were outside acceptable ranges, As a result, they sent her home.

We returned on Wednesday, and they took new labs. Those results showed that only 10 of the measurable items were outside of normal ranges, and of those, only two were significant. As a result, she was able to receive her third chemo treatment. Immediately after finishing her treatment, we went across the street to Princess Anne Hospital to have her PET scan. This afternoon we returned to the oncologist, Dr. Lee, to review her PET scan and discuss the next phase of treatment.

When we realized this meeting would take place on Good

Friday, we knew it was no accident. Our GOD did not disappoint. From Mildred's skull to her thighs, her scan showed no evidence of any malignant glucose activity. If there are any cancer cells present, they are too small to be detected by today's technology. Once again, she is *cancer-free*. For the third time, God has removed the cancer from her body. I don't care how many times her body is attacked; He will heal her.

During this past month, Mildred had one of her "meetings" with our Heavenly Father where He told her she still had much work to do, and He would let her know when it was time to come *home*. I continue to be amazed at what God has done. I have had the privilege to personally be part of three miracles. I have read the reports and discussed her status with our first oncologist, Dr. Steinberg, and now our second oncologist, Dr. Lee. In both cases, they were stunned and admitted that their medical training could not give them adequate words to fully explain her results. Neither of them quite knows what to make of her, but I do, and so do her nurses. There is only one explanation—*God reigns*! As we celebrate this Easter weekend, mere words are inadequate for me to properly thank Him. I can only say *thank you* and give Him all the glory, for He is truly God!

Day 1,026 PC
Another Bump

May 8, 2015

HE IS RISEN INDEED

I was admitted to the hospital again in late February 2015 for a viral infection. One part of the tests and procedures they did was updated CT scans. The doctors told my husband, Bob, that the scans showed the cancer had come back and was raging. It took Bob five or six hours before he could tell me what they said. I told him that night that I did not care what the tests showed; I was going to continue to stay with my Heavenly Father.

It took me until Sunday night to process this latest piece of information. I realized then that I did not have to accept this because my Heavenly Father told me He was taking care of it. I have continued to ask Him what He wanted me to do on this journey. That night, Sunday night, He told me to quit asking Him what He wanted me to do. He would let me know when the time was right. Approximately five to 10 minutes later, it started snowing and sleeting in my hospital room, and the snow was gold. I thought I had lost my mind. Bob had left the hospital to go home and take care of the dogs when the snow and sleet happened. When

> he came back to see me, he told me I was going to be healed on Good Friday. He said that something told him to look at the calendar while he was home. I was scheduled to have another PET scan on Good Friday and then meet with the oncologist.
>
> When we met with the doctor on Good Friday, there was no evidence of any active cancer in my body. I had told my sister about the vision I had seen, and she said God had healed me that night. Our life group usually meets at our house on Tuesday nights. I was so dumbfounded about what I had seen while I was in the hospital that I asked my life group about it, and no one had any answers. I found it absolutely amazing that this happened, and I was told on Good Friday that I did not have any active cancer. My family and friends celebrated with me by attending Good Friday services. I remember Linda telling me that I had a halo around my head that night.

Other than having to be infused with fluids on certain days after receiving chemo, Mildred has had a good month. She becomes fatigued on some days, but relatively speaking, she is doing well and maintaining her normal levels after each chemo treatment. Her most recent treatment was on Monday, April 27th, and she was doing okay until early this Friday morning. At approximately 3:00 a.m., she awoke in a puddle of vomit in her bed, some of which she ingested. For approximately the next six hours, she vomited and experienced diarrhea and coughing with a congested fluid sound. She was scheduled to go to the oncologist's office that morning to receive more fluids, so I took her there before her scheduled appointment. They took her vital signs and immediately recommended she go to the Princess Anne Hospital ER across the street.

Upon arriving at the ER, Mildred's heart rate was 125 beats per minute, her oxygen level was 91, her body temperature was more than 100, and she was still experiencing diarrhea and coughing. They immediately did blood work and X-rays. They found that her blood glucose, hemoglobin, and potassium levels were very low, and she had pneumonia, most likely caused by ingesting her vomit. They put her on oxygen and began infusing her with antibiotics and fluids. After about an hour of treatment, they admitted her and took her upstairs. They continued to treat her for the next five hours or so, at which point they took new blood draws. Thankfully, her glucose, hemoglobin, and potassium levels had begun to rise, although they were still below the normal ranges. Her heart rate had declined to 93, which is still higher than normal but improving. Her body temperature had come down to 98.1 and her oxygen rate had improved to 97. The only negative sign was that her blood pressure had dropped to 91/54, and she still had diarrhea. The doctors recommended continuing to monitor all these levels and treating her with antibiotics and fluids.

While this is yet another bump in the road, we will overcome it as we have the many others. Our Father continues to walk beside us and carry us when necessary. He also brings others into our lives who we have been blessed to minister to and pray for. We had the opportunity this past Tuesday to meet a couple (Cecil and Barbara) who were former missionaries in Fiji. They have been back in the States for a number of years, and Cecil has been a caregiver to his wife who has progressively worsening dementia. He is in the early stages of treatment for Stage 3 pancreatic cancer. We were able to bless them with food, Mildred's inspirational story, and prayer. We will assist them in every way we can through our Voices of Hope ministry and help meet their spiritual, emotional, and physical needs. Our experiences are still enabling us to bless and minister to others who have not been as fortunate as we have been. We thank our Heavenly Father for all He has done and continues to do. Please lift up Cecil and Barbara to our Heavenly Father and ask Him to pour down blessings and healing upon them. May they be as blessed as we have been.

Day 1,029 PC

Home Again

May 11, 2015

Mildred was able to come home today. Her numbers have continued to improve, so the doctor said she could go home as long as she takes the antibiotics and rests. Although that is not something she likes to do, she has promised to do it this week. She has to visit the doctor on Wednesday afternoon for a follow-up. I certainly did not expect her to come home today. Once more, God has demonstrated His power of healing and love. We thank each of you and ask that you continue to pray for Cecil and Barabara as well.

Day 1,085 PC

The Journey Continues

July 6, 2015

It has been almost two months since I last posted because Mildred has been doing very well since the oncologist started the new round of chemo on three-week intervals. She has not experienced any significant side effects from the first two treatments. She received her third treatment on Monday, June 22nd and seemed to be doing well again. She received her injection and fluids that week and seemed to be fine. However, in the week of June 29th, she began experiencing severe diarrhea. They gave her a prescription med to get it under control and also decided to give her four days of fluids to counteract the dehydration that diarrhea brings. The diarrhea seemed to be under control by Saturday when she stayed home and rested. Yesterday morning, July 5th, she awoke and, while feeling a little tired, went for her fluid IV. All seemed to be heading in the right direction until about 5:30 yesterday afternoon when she began vomiting. For the next three hours, she vomited and complained of severe abdominal pain. After trying to calm things down with over-the-counter medicine to no avail, we went to the Princess Anne Hospital ER.

Despite a typical crowded holiday weekend at the ER, they were able to get her into a room within an hour. They ran blood work and a urine specimen and eventually a contrast CT scan. After getting the results, the ER doctor sat down with us and told us her gallbladder was infected and needed to be removed. They admitted her to the medical surgical floor and began pumping her full of antibiotics.

The standard treatment for gallbladder surgery is to fill the patient with antibiotics for at least 24 hours and then surgically remove the gallbladder.

Despite the ER doctor's rush to surgery, the consensus of Mildred's surgeon and oncologist was to treat the gallbladder with a combination of antibiotics for at least the next 48 hours. They hope to see progress that will allow them to avoid operating to remove her gallbladder. Given her higher-than-normal risk factors, they want to avoid surgery if at all possible. She is still having a high level of pain when she is awake, but the pain medicine knocks her out for a couple hours at a time and enables her to get some rest. The doctors did say there is no evidence of cancer in her gallbladder and that she probably would have had this occur even if she did not have cancer.

While the last two months have probably been the most "normal" time we have had on this journey, the journey still continues. Once again, we have another bump in the road to overcome, but we remain confident that our Father will continue to walk with us. I would be lying if I said I was not tired, but I pray every day when my eyes open for His strength and wisdom in me and His continued healing of Mildred. We remain steadfast in our belief that all this has been for a purpose, and that purpose is being fulfilled through our Voices of Hope ministry to others.

We will not quit. We will not run from the challenge. We will continue to march forward with our Father by our side.

Day 1,087 PC

Heading in the Right Direction

July 8, 2015

Mildred remains in the hospital with the gallbladder infection, and they continue to infuse her with antibiotics. She has less pain than when she was admitted Sunday evening. The only time she is really in pain is when she gets out of bed to use the bathroom. Other than that, the pain is manageable thanks to the pain medicine. Her doctors expect her to remain hospitalized for a few more days.

I pray that our Father will touch her with His healing hands and bring her home without having surgery. I also pray and ask each of you to pray for Winston, another cancer patient and friend of ours who is having emergency surgery tomorrow due to blood clots and bleeding. He has been on chemo for close to a year, and they had to begin radiation on Monday due to the ineffectiveness of the chemo. May our loving Father embrace Winston and his wife, Pennie, and bring them healing and peace.

Day 1,089 PC

Prayer Works!

July 10, 2015

I was able to spend some time at the hospital this morning with Mildred. She is doing very well, considering where she was on Monday. The doctors are encouraged but want to see her numbers stay in the normal ranges for at least a couple days before sending her home. At this point, surgery is no longer a topic of discussion. She is her normal self in terms of alertness and color. We enjoyed spending a couple hours together.

In the same vein, Winston came through his surgery very well. He is able to move about without any significant pain issues. We give thanks to our God for answering all the prayers that were put forth for both Mildred and Winston.

May they both rest in His loving and healing arms.

Day 1,096 PC

A Relapse

July 17, 2015

Despite feeling relatively normal and regaining her strength at home on Tuesday and Wednesday, Mildred awoke on Thursday not feeling well. As the morning progressed into the afternoon, the most recent symptoms of vomiting and abdominal pain returned. I took her to the ER in the afternoon, and they admitted her. She again received antibiotics and pain meds after her labs and X-rays. By the time I left the hospital around midnight, she was feeling better but still weak. The ER doctor spoke with her surgeon who was on call last night. The plan is for her surgeon to speak with her oncologist today and decide whether to remove her gallbladder, despite the fact that she is a high-risk surgical candidate. In the alternative, they could insert a biliary drain into her gallbladder.

Please continue to lift her up in prayer. She really needs our

Father's loving arms of strength and healing today. Last night was one of the few times I heard Mildred say she is getting tired. I will continue to press forward on this journey with our Father and pray that the combination of both of us and all of you will be sufficient to lift her up and heal her.

Day 1,097 PC

Decision Time

July 18, 2015

I spent most of the day with Mildred at the hospital. They continued to give her antibiotics and pain meds to get things under control. Fortunately, the pain meds pretty much eliminated her pain. She still has a little discomfort, but she is back to where she was on Tuesday and Wednesday. All things considered, we have been very blessed.

We had the chance to speak with the surgeon, the hospital attending physician, and the oncologist today. All agree that simply treating her with antibiotics and sending her home will not solve the real problem. Her gallbladder will continue to be inflamed and infected without any serious intervention. We discussed both options with each of the doctors, and they discussed the options with each other. Unfortunately, as sometimes happens, there is no clear consensus.

The oncologist says definitely take it out now, that she has not had chemo in four weeks and would be able to resume chemo in two or three weeks, removing only one drug from her chemo mix. The drain approach presents issues for her getting chemo since she would in essence have an open wound that could become negatively affected by the chemo. The surgeon leans toward surgery—do it initially using a laparoscopic method but recognize that once they begin, they may have to cut her open if they encounter any problems. There are definitely risks (compromised immune system, bleeding out, etc.), but a successful procedure would solve her problem instead of prolonging it. The attending physician believes the biliary drain procedure would be the best option. It is the least invasive of the two, and she can always have the gallbladder removed later if it becomes necessary. There is, however, a tube with an exterior bag to collect waste. The bag will have to be emptied once a day or more.

Mildred and I have discussed the options and have a few additional questions we will ask tomorrow. We expect to arrive at a decision then. In the meantime, we will pray and ask each of you to pray for God's wisdom, guidance, and healing. He will reveal to us what we should do. *His time . . . His plan.*

Day 1,099 PC

Decision Made

July 20, 2015

In the last 24 hours, Mildred's abdominal pain and vomiting have come back. They tried putting her on a bland, soft diet beginning Sunday at lunch, but by Sunday evening, the symptoms returned. After additional conversations with her doctors and a lot of prayer, we made the decision last night to have the biliary drain inserted. The majority opinion of her doctors is that her gallbladder is too infected and inflamed to attempt to remove it right now. Their priority, particularly in light of the last 24 hours, is to get it under control. By inserting the tube, the belief is that it will provide a conduit for the bile and waste to exit her body instead of accumulating and continuing to cause more infection. How long she will need to have the tube is an unknown at this point. It could be weeks; it could be months. Her gallbladder has a perforation that will eventually have to be dealt with and will most likely result in its removal, but the immediate priority is to eliminate the infection. We are currently waiting to hear back from her surgeon for an exact time for the procedure, but their hope is to perform it today.

While this procedure is less risky than removal, it still carries some risk given her existing health and condition. We pray that our Father will hold her in His loving arms, give wisdom to the medical professionals, and heal her body. We covet your prayers.

Day 1,100 PC

He Continues to Amaze

July 21, 2015

The procedure to insert a drain tube in her gallbladder was performed this afternoon. The doctor said it went well. Mildred now has a tube implanted in her gallbladder that exits the right side of her body and connects to a bag where her bile is collected. What the doctor said amazed Mildred and me and served as further evidence of our Father's love for us and how much He is walking with us on this journey. When the doctor went in to insert the tube, he found that a third gallstone (everyone thought she only had two) had exited the gallbladder, traveled through the gallbladder's bile duct, and gone into the main duct that transports bile from both the liver and the gallbladder. That stone had become lodged where the main bile duct meets the small intestine and was blocking the flow of bile. As a result, her bile was backing up into her gallbladder and causing it to swell and become infected. Think of an enema bag filled with water and squeezing it but having the end tip of the hose blocked. Every time you squeeze the bag, nothing comes out, and it only increases the pressure on the bag. That is what was happening to Mildred. The drain tube will prevent this from happening. More importantly, the third stone can be removed by a gastrointestinal doctor as outpatient surgery in his office. Once that is done, Mildred can return to the hospital to have the drain tube removed, and her gallbladder should function normally.

Once again, mere words are inadequate. Three weeks ago we had no idea she had this problem. She spent the better part of the last two weeks in the hospital, and we were fearful she would undergo major surgery with major risks. Instead, our Father, as He has all along, *has this*! This is just another bump in the road on our journey. We give God all the praise and glory. We have been so blessed, and we pray that we are able to share His blessings with others.

Day 1,101 PC

One More

July 22, 2015

The surgeon and his PA checked on Mildred this morning. The feeling is that she is doing so well that they are going to schedule the procedure for tomorrow to remove the newfound gallstone that is the source of the problem. Since she is already in the hospital and came through yesterday's procedure so well, they want to get it done now. Once it is removed, she will need the tube and bag for about six weeks in order for everything to heal properly, and then it can be removed. What *joyous news*! Our God is *truly awesome*!

Day 1,102 PC

It's Out

July 23, 2015

Mildred had the second procedure this morning that removed the gallstone blocking the flow of her bile. The surgeon said all went well, and there were no issues. His expectation is that she will be able to come home sometime this weekend. In approximately six weeks she can have the drain tube removed. She is scheduled to have her next PET scan on Monday, and we meet with the oncologist on Friday, July 31st to discuss the results and plan her next phase of treatment. We expect continued good news as we have much to accomplish. It seems our Father is bringing more people to us so we can expand our reach. We thank each of you for your prayers and love.

Day 1,105 PC

So Blessed

July 26, 2015

Mildred was able to come home Friday afternoon. I had to work at the salon all day Friday and Saturday, so I could not take care of her as I wanted to. However, Lisa, one of our friends and fellow life group members, was at the hospital on Friday to visit Mildred and was there when the doctor said Mildred could go home. She offered to take her home and get her settled. I had the clothes Mildred needed to go home in, and Daniella, one of the girls in the salon, offered to take them to the hospital and help Mildred get changed. Lisa took Mildred home, got her settled, and bought some fresh food for her to eat. The next morning, Mildred's sister, Marie, came to the house, prepared food for Mildred, did some housecleaning (not my strength), and spent the morning with her.

How blessed we were. Mildred and I talked last night how we cannot imagine where we would be on this journey were it not for everyone's outpouring of support and love. We thank each of you for all you have done and pray that we are able to do the same for many others in the future.

Day 1,110 PC

Not Even a Bump Anymore

July 31, 2015

Mildred has been resting at home the last few days since being discharged from the hospital. She is regaining her strength and has been eager to get out and about. Today, we met with Dr. Lee, her oncologist, to discuss her recent gallbladder issue and her most recent PET scan. His thoughts on the biliary drain connected to her gallbladder is that if the healing continues at its current pace, they may be able to remove it in three weeks.

The PET scan from Monday showed that a few of the previous cancer lesions in her lungs have begun to grow again. When we considered that she has not had any chemo treatments for six weeks, as well as everything else that has occurred, this is hardly anything to worry about. She will not be able to receive chemo again until the drain is removed, which is another reason her oncologist would like to see it come out in three weeks.

Our takeaway from today's and recent events is that they are not even bumps in the road anymore. In the early stages of our journey, we probably would have been concerned by the events of the past few days and weeks, but not anymore. We realize that we will be engaged in battle on this journey for the remainder of our lives. There will be other bumps in the road, but we also know that *He's got it*! He continues to give us both the strength each day to confront the challenges we will encounter, and there will be challenges. However, it is from these challenges that we are able to grow in *faith*. Hopefully, we are able to inspire others who are on their own journeys. Whether it is health issues, family issues, financial issues, or whatever, He will not leave us or forsake us. In fact, if we rest in His care, there are times when He will pick us up and literally carry us.

May each of you be as blessed as we have been these past three-plus years.

Day 1,136 PC

Perspective

August 26, 2015

Over the last five days, we have visited with Mildred's surgeon who oversaw the installation of the biliary tube and drain, as well as her oncologist. The surgeon examined her drain, pronounced it in good shape, and said he did not see any reason it could not be removed. We are waiting to hear a definite day and time for the procedure.

Today, Mildred had her normal lab work done, and then we visited with Dr. Lee. All her lab results were in the normal ranges, and she is slowly gaining weight, currently weighing in at 114 pounds. Her tumor markers (CEA) that are measured in her blood have increased to 61. While this is higher than the 20 to 35 range it has been in, there is little reason to be concerned. Her CEA was 400+ on the day she was diagnosed. She will begin chemo again on September 8th and return to her regular three-week treatment intervals. The doctors feel that once she gets back on her chemo regimen, her CEA will begin to decline again, and the cancer cells that have started growing will once again be diminished, if not eradicated.

While at the oncologist's office, we saw some other patients we have come to know. Carrie, the 40-year-old mother, was one of them. She was with her mother, Sylvia. Carrie's breast cancer had now reached the final stages. She is on oxygen 24/7 and has suffered significant weight loss. After having surgery, radiation, and chemo, she has now been told that those are no longer viable treatment options. She has been reduced to trying healing oils, specific vitamins, and other long-shot methods. In addition, her 43-year-old brother died of a massive heart attack on July 23rd. It was quite a lot for her and her mother to handle.

Many people we have crossed paths with have passed on. Why our Father has chosen to bless us, we do not know. Only He can answer that. Do we believe He has given us a purpose? *Absolutely!* Are we deserving of such grace and blessings? No more than any other believer. What we do know is that we are thankful for each and every day. As we reflect on the events of this day, we give Him thanks. We pray for Carrie, Sylvia, and their families. We pray for each of you that all will find peace in His loving arms.

Tell someone you care about how much you love them today. None of us knows whether tomorrow will give us another opportunity to do so.

Day 1,145 PC

Déjà Vu

September 4, 2015

Mildred had the drain tube removed from her gallbladder this past Monday. Everything checked out fine, and she had normal days on

Monday and Tuesday. However, around 4:00 a.m. on Wednesday, she awoke writhing in agony and screaming in pain. Mildred has a high tolerance for pain, so I knew she was in extreme pain. I took her to the ER where they did blood work and an ultrasound. All her blood work was normal, but the ultrasound showed that her gallbladder was inflamed and enlarged. Nothing showed a direct cause for her pain. Her bile flow was normal, and there was no evidence of any stones. They gave her pain and nausea meds intravenously and then sent her home. The meds lessened the pain, but it was still at an above-normal level. The doctor thought that since she ate foods, she should not have the day before—fried chicken, taco chips with salsa—the gallbladder may have had an adverse reaction.

After coming home, she rested in her recliner and slept in her bed the rest of Wednesday and all of Thursday while taking pain meds every four hours. When she awoke Friday morning, the pain was still at the same level, so she returned to the ER where she was seen by the same doctor that saw her on Wednesday. Aside from blood work, they did a more detailed, higher resolution scan with color-coded dye. The consensus of the ER doctor, the surgeon who had inserted the drain tube, and her oncologist was that the drain tube needed to be reinserted.

Late this afternoon, they performed the procedure and reinserted the drain tube. The expectation is that this will allow the inflammation to subside and remove any infection. It will also allow her to restart her chemo as long as she has physically recovered her strength. Her chemo right now is scheduled for this Tuesday, but it is possible it may be pushed back a few days, depending on her condition. Since she has not had any chemo since June 22nd, the medical opinion is that this is a higher priority when the inflammation and infection in her gallbladder have subsided. They plan to keep her in the hospital at least the next couple of days until the gallbladder has returned to normal, which hopefully it will.

While I do not want to minimize her condition, this is yet another bump in the road. So long as our Father continues to give us strength, we will continue marching forward. *We will not retreat or surrender!* No matter what comes at us, we will stay on this journey. God has healed Mildred every time before, and He will again. Our faith rests in Him!

Day 1,149 PC
Home Again

September 8, 2015

Mildred was able to come home from the hospital last night. She still has a slightly higher level of pain than normal, but the infection appears to be gone, the drain tube is flowing as intended, and all her blood and lab numbers are good. She is still somewhat tired, which led to the postponement of her chemo originally scheduled for today. The plan is for her to rest at home the next few days, regain her strength, and then decide if she is able to handle receiving chemo sometime next week. We just keep moving forward one day at a time.

Day 1,158 PC
The Mountain and the Valley

September 17, 2015

Mildred spent most of last week resting and recovering at home from the new drain tube they inserted. For the most part, she had a good week and is regaining her strength.

Last weekend, we were blessed to have our ministry, Voices of Hope, and us recognized in our weekend church services. We had a table set up with our information flyers and copies of a previous magazine article about us. We were blessed to speak with so many people with various experiences. These conversations led to people who were either cancer survivors and want to serve in our ministry or cancer patients who were in need of the services our ministry can provide. Other individuals spoke with us and took our information for further prayer and consideration. Our Father continues to open doors for Voices of Hope to expand and reach more and more people. Wherever He leads us, we will follow. It is truly a joy to be able to bless others who have been or are on their own cancer journey. We eagerly await His guidance.

Earlier today, we met with our oncologist and reviewed the events of the past couple months concerning Mildred's gallbladder. She has not had chemo treatments since June 22nd. Dr. Lee's and the surgeon's opinion is that the tube and bag should remain in place. They believe that the tube will enable her gallbladder to function normally. As long as the gallbladder is normal, she should be able to receive chemo. So the full chemo treatment was resumed this morning. We continue our journey with our Father to the mountaintop.

One of the emotionally difficult parts of doing ministry is the relationships we build with cancer patients who are truly in the valley. As I write this, I ask each of you to pray fervently for Carrie, the young woman we have written about before who is battling breast cancer. Carrie is now taking chemo in pill form and also receiving radiation. She remains on oxygen 24/7. She is a fighter and will not give up, but ultimately the remainder of her journey is in God's hands. Please pray that He will provide healing for her and strength for her mother, Sylvia, who is her constant caregiver. Pray that He will take her two children into His loving embrace and give Mildred and me the words to help bring them peace.

Day 1,164 PC

Another Bump

September 23, 2015

Mildred received the full complement of chemo last Thursday. The first two days she did all right, receiving fluids each day along with her steroid pill she normally takes after chemo for three days. But Sunday afternoon she began to display the side effects of chemo. By Monday morning she was vomiting, had chills, felt miserable, had diarrhea, and so on. In addition, the fluid draining into the gallbladder drain tube and bag began to discolor from mostly clear to dark brown. On Tuesday, she again received fluids and an IV that stopped her from vomiting. However, as the day wore on, she continued to worsen. Early this morning I took her to the ER. After performing a battery of tests and a CT scan, they found a bacterial infection in her urine, in the drain tube fluid, and in the drain tube itself. They do not have the CT scan results back yet, but the attending physician's initial diagnosis is that the gallbladder is again infected. It is also possible that the infection has spread to other areas, but they will not know until they see the CT scan results. They admitted her immediately into the hospital and begun pumping her full of antibiotics. The attending physician plans to speak with her oncologist and surgeon once the CT scan results are in, which should be in the morning. Surgery is again on the table as a treatment option, particularly if the infection has spread to additional areas besides the gallbladder.

As I write this, I do not have any clear thought path as to what will happen to her. Surgery has been previously labeled a life-or-death option, yet having reoccurring infections is not a viable treatment plan. I can only do as we have done from the beginning—give it to God. He has had this all along, and He still does. I trust that He will heal her in whatever way He chooses. His ways are not for me to understand, only to believe. Tonight I ask for your prayers. You have been there with us throughout, and as we encounter yet another bump in the road, it is your prayers and His love that will carry us through.

Day 1,165 PC

What Now?

September 24, 2015

Mildred is doing better. The multitude of antibiotics has reduced the infection but not yet eliminated it. The surgeon replaced her existing drain tube and bag with new ones today, so one source of infection was eliminated. Her CT scan results did not indicate the presence of infection anywhere other than her gallbladder. They are waiting for some of the blood cultures to mature so they can be sure exactly what type(s) of bacterial infection she has and better match the antibiotics to it.

The most significant question that remains unanswered is what can be done to prevent infection from reoccurring. While there are certainly no guarantees when you have an open wound with a drain tube running into your abdominal cavity, I have asked each of the medical professionals to think outside the box for solutions. A gallbladder drain tube is normally intended as a short-term fix for a gallbladder problem. The conventional solution is to remove the gallbladder once the inflammation and infection have resolved. However, in Mildred's case, surgery is such a high-risk proposition that leaving a functioning drain tube in place long-term is more preferable. My thought is that whether it involves methods to better sanitize the wound, bypass the gallbladder while leaving it in her, reroute the discharge fluid, or develop a long-term regimen of drugs to combat infection, there must be a way to minimize infection and inflammation while leaving the tube and bag in place. We hope to have some options to review by next week. In the meantime, she will continue to receive antibiotics and rest for the next few days.

Again, we thank each of you for your prayers, and I pray that our Father will continue to keep Mildred in His loving embrace and impart wisdom and knowledge to her physicians.

Day 1,169 PC
A Difficult Day

September 28, 2015

After spending the last five days in the hospital, Mildred finally was able to come home this afternoon. Although she is home, she will continue receiving antibiotics intravenously for the next seven days. We will find out in the morning whether a nurse will come to the house to administer the IV or if we need to go to the outpatient infusion center each day. My guess is that it will be at the infusion center due to insurance. Mildred is certainly better than she was when she was admitted but is still not back to her normal level. Hopefully, over the next seven days she will improve and regain her strength.

Despite being released from the hospital, today was a difficult day. We found out from Sylvia that Carrie passed away last week while Mildred was in the hospital. Carrie fought as hard as she could, but in the end, her cancer was just too much. Our hearts ache for her mother, Sylvia, who has now buried two children in the last few months. Her pain is unfathomable and will only increase as Carrie's husband plans to sell the house, take the kids, and move to the West Coast. We pray that she will find peace in our Father's loving arms.

The most difficult part of life is when someone so young leaves us. I know it happens throughout life, but I think when it does, it shakes our faith more than anything else. Whether it is a child or a young adult, we just do not expect someone who is young to die. When it happens, we ask our Father why. To be honest, I don't have an answer. I know when my father died after succumbing to MS at the age of 34, I struggled at the young age of 13 to accept it. There is hardly a day that goes by that I do not think about him and wonder why God chose him so early. Why has God chosen Carrie and left behind two young children without a mother? I think situations such as these are the crux of our faith because there is no other way to handle it but to accept it. We are unable to answer why. We can only say that our Father loves us and that we put our faith in Him and pray that He will give us peace.

CARRIE

In three plus years of this journey, my Heavenly Father has stopped the cancer three times. He is my healer. I learned today that my friend Carrie went home to be with our Savior. I met Carrie and her mom in the treatment room. I was supposed to get my chemo on Monday, but since it was Labor Day weekend, I did not. I think my Heavenly Father wanted me to meet Carrie on Wednesday instead. It was all set up by Him. When I went to the treatment room, some friends there wanted to talk with me. After I talked with them, I sat down in my regular chair, the one I sat in when I first met Anthony. Carrie was sitting in the chair that Anthony had sat in.

Something told me to speak with her, so I did. Carrie introduced herself, and I thought she said her name was Terry. I did not understand at first what Carrie's mom was saying due to her thick accent. At that moment, Carrie received a phone call. While she was speaking on the phone, her mother began to talk to me. She told me how angry she had been with God. She said she was angry because Carrie was her baby daughter. She had two sons, but Carrie was her baby girl. She was very angry that Carrie had cancer. Carrie's mom told me that one night she went to bed, and something woke her up. She went downstairs, opened her Bible randomly, and God began to answer her questions. God asked her why she was angry. She said God walked her through different pages in the Bible, and when she was through, He had answered all her questions. She was no longer angry with God. I said to her, "Thank God you are no longer angry with Him."

Shortly after, Carrie finished her phone call. I then began to talk with Carrie. Her mother said Carrie was having a hard time because she had breast cancer. The doctors had previously told her that her cancer was shrinking, but six weeks later they told her the cancer was growing again. She was very depressed. Carrie had a five-year-old daughter and a husband she was very concerned about. I talked to her and was able to tell her what God had done and was continuing to do for me. He could do the same for her. She just needed to have faith and trust in Him.

After I finished speaking with her, Carrie finished her chemo treatment. At that time, my chemo treatments lasted six hours, so she was finished before I was. Carrie thanked me, told me she was supposed to meet me today, and that my words had made her feel so much better. She then hugged me, and I asked her if I could have her phone number so I could keep in touch with her and her mom. When she gave me the piece of paper with their names and numbers on it, the words that came out of my mouth were, "Oh my God." Her mother's name was Sylvia and the daughter's name was Carrie. I have a sister who lives in Portland, Oregon, named Sylvia. I also have a sister who lives in Jacksonville, Florida, named Carrie. Their names were spelled exactly like my two sisters. That is why I say it was a God thing that we met because how many times are you going to meet two people in life at the same time that have the same names as your two sisters?

Carrie was only 37 years old. She was a young, beautiful lady who left behind a beautiful little five-year-old girl. Two months before she left this world, she lost her brother to a massive heart attack. My heart aches for her mom. The pain of losing two of your children within two months of each other when they are young adults is almost impossible to understand. These last months on my own journey have become increasingly difficult because I have lost so many friends I met on this journey. At least they have all gone to be with our Heavenly Father.

Day 1,186 PC
Another Difficult Day

October 15, 2015

Today was one of those days we encounter on this journey that truly leaves our emotions in disarray. Early this morning we received news that another of our fellow travelers had succumbed to this dreaded disease. Winston, our friend and soulmate, had fought the gallant fight for close to two years. He initially battled cancer in his kidneys, but by the end, it had spread throughout his bone marrow. Mercifully, our Father took him home so he would be free of the pain and suffering he had endured for so long. Our prayers and love are with his wife, Pennie, and their adult children. We will gather on Tuesday to celebrate his life and his final victory in our Father's kingdom.

Later in the morning, Mildred and I met with her surgeon to discuss our options and develop a plan for her ongoing gallbladder problem. Over the past three months, she has been hospitalized numerous times for infection in her gallbladder. They have treated it with antibiotics and inserted drain tubes in an attempt to overcome the infection. While the doctors have had some degree of success for short periods of time, the gallbladder continues to be a source of infection and further weakening of her body.

Over the past three months, she has only been able to receive one chemo treatment a few weeks ago. While that treatment did result in reducing some of her markers, the cancer has grown. The longer the gallbladder remains in her body, the weaker her body will become and the more the cancer will grow without chemo.

The surgeon indicated that at this point there are no other options to resolve the gallbladder issue than surgery. If the gallbladder is not surgically removed, it is just a matter of time before the cancer overtakes her. He also reminded us that the surgery has significant risks, and he may take a "look-see" and decide that her gallbladder and surrounding organs such as her liver and kidneys are so far gone that it does not justify proceeding. There is also the possibility that she may not survive the procedure, given her many surgeries as far back as her teens and 20s with her hysterectomy to now with her initial colon surgery accompanied by cancer.

After he finished explaining the risks, he asked for our decision—a go or no go. We had prayed about this for these past few weeks. We believe that our Father will clearly guide the surgeon's hands and mind during this procedure and that the procedure will be successful. We do understand the risks, but our Father put us on this journey for a purpose. We still have much work to do to complete the tasks He has given us, and He does not intend for this journey to end here. Our surgeon is also a man of faith, and we do not believe that is an accident. Our Father has surrounded us throughout this journey with people of faith to guide us and help us. He has communicated with us through visions as well. When all is said and done, this gallbladder will be just another bump in the road as we continue on the path He has put before us.

We gave the surgeon the go-ahead to remove Mildred's gallbladder. Mildred will need some preliminary lab work, an EKG, and X-rays the early part of next week. Assuming nothing unexpected appears on any of them, the surgery will be sometime in the week of October 26th. If they are able to do the procedure laparoscopically, she will be in the hospital for two days, including the day of surgery. If they have to open her up, she will probably be in the hospital for a week. Either way, once she is discharged, she will have approximately one month of recovery time before she can resume her normal, everyday life. We look forward to that day. In the meantime, we will keep on marching. We ask each of you to continue marching with us through your continued prayers.

We also ask that you include Pennie and her family in your prayers. While we will miss seeing our friend Winston, we know where he now resides. Let us not say goodbye to him but rather until we meet again.

WINSTON AND ANNETTE

Today was another one of those hard days where I lost another friend. Winston went home today. You miss all the friends and think about each of their journeys and how it was for them. I am still marching on my journey as hard as I can. One night I was asking my Father what He wanted me to do. He told me to stop asking Him, that I still have lots of work to do. He will let me know when the time is right. Since then I have continued trying to work with other patients and helping others along the way by bringing them meals, taking them to and from medical appointments, and just being with them while they are on their own journeys. It seems to help them to know they are not alone. Some people will open up to you, while others want you to stay quiet. I have learned that if you can stay with them on their journey for a while, it seems like they begin to trust and open up a little bit. They will tell you something that is very

> small but seems very big to them. Annette was like that. She worked at our church and kept her cancer a secret from almost everyone around her. She was called home 11 days before Winston.

Day 1,192 PC

Waiting

October 21, 2015

Yesterday we attended the celebration service for our friend and fellow traveler, Winston. The service was truly a celebration of his life as told by his family and friends. Mildred and I both talked afterwards that we would want her service, whenever the time comes, to not only be a celebration of her life but also a celebration of our Father and His presence in her life. There would be plenty of singing, dancing, and speaking as we share in the joy of her life. It will truly be a time of praise and worship, not sadness and grief.

Mildred's gallbladder surgery has been scheduled for 7:30 a.m. on Tuesday, November 10th. The surgeon had hoped to schedule it sooner, but he wants a second surgeon in the OR with him, and this was the earliest date they would both be available. His thinking, which we agree with, is that in case anything starts to go wrong, a second set of trained hands with experience could be the difference between life and death. We know our Father will be there to guide them both.

Mildred continues to rest at home. She has not been able to regain the strength she had prior to the onset of the gallbladder issues, but she is doing okay. Her weight has dropped to 103, and she drinks a lot of fluids to remain hydrated. While the last few weeks have been difficult and challenging, we continue to rest in His love and care. *He's still got it!*

> ### THE GALLBLADDER
>
> For the past few months I have been dealing with an issue with my gallbladder. It keeps getting infected. The doctors have tried to heal the infection with antibiotics, but the infection keeps coming back. I had a biliary tube put in, but it does not seem to help very much. Today we met with the surgeon to discuss removing my gallbladder. No one really wants to operate on it because it could be very dangerous for me. No one seems to have positive thoughts about this operation. So today, while the surgeon was speaking to us about his thoughts, I stopped him. I told him the Lord would guide his hands, the Lord would do the operation, and everything would be okay. I did not want to hear another negative thought about the operation I am going to have in two weeks. Sometimes life by itself can be very negative. When you continue to hear negative thoughts over and over again, it is as if someone is pulling the inside of your stomach out, especially when you are a positive person. I think of myself as a positive person, so it is hard when I am around someone with nothing but negative things to say. On this journey, I will not do or say anything that is not

positive—for myself, for others, and for all the people who are on their own journeys.

I hope that when people look at me, they can say that I am a positive person. On this journey, you have to make yourself be positive because there is so much that is not positive when you are going through chemo, when you see your friends going through chemo and all of the side effects that everyone suffers. Sometimes you have to make yourself laugh. Even for the smallest thing, you have to put laughter into it because it helps keep you going every day. I just keep putting one foot in front of the other, and I keep marching. So with my positive attitude, I will march on, have the surgery, and get rid of this gallbladder once and for all. As my husband keeps saying, "It's just another bump in the road."

HARRIET AND BOB

Today while I was at the surgeon's office, I ran into Harriet and Bob, long-time clients of the salon. Bob had been told approximately six weeks ago that he has cancer. They both looked good. Harriet said she is taking it one day at a time. I asked if I could stop by to see them, and they said I could. I want to talk with Bob. Since I have cancer, I thought he may want to talk with someone who has been through it. I also would like to talk with him because I am not sure if he knows my Heavenly Father. They had a really hard time

> when they were first told that Bob has cancer. I still think they are having a hard time dealing with it, but if I can help them, I would like to do that. Shortly after I saw Harriett and Bob, I learned that he had passed away.

Day 1,206 PC
In Need of His Loving Embrace

November 4, 2015

Six days from now, Mildred is scheduled to have surgery to remove her gallbladder. As anyone reading this knows, the risks are significant. While the procedure will begin laparoscopically, the likelihood is that the surgeons will have to open her up. Once that happens, there are two possible outcomes. They successfully remove the gallbladder, she spends a week in the hospital, and then she has a four-week recovery period at home. The second possibility is that she departs this world. Both outcomes have a relatively even chance of occurring. While death has been a constant companion on our journey, only one other time have we had to face the immediacy of death—when she first began chemo treatment and her esophagus and interior linings were severely burned by the chemo back in October 2012. While cancer may eventually claim her, it has always been "down the road." The cancer has never reached a point where it was only a matter of a few days before she died.

We have believed and said from the beginning that our Father put us on this journey for a purpose—to minister to others. We still believe that. However, I would be less than truthful if I did not acknowledge an element of fear regarding Tuesday. I know God has this, but that does not mean the outcome will be as I wish. While I continue to pray every day that God will guide the surgeon's hands and mind and heal her, I believe there is strength in numbers. Therefore, I am asking everyone and anyone to pray for Mildred. Specifically pray with one loud, unified voice on Monday evening, November 9th between the hours of 7:00 and 8:00 p.m. Eastern Standard Time. We will be conducting a prayer service at our house during that time, and anyone, regardless of church affiliation or no affiliation, is welcome to attend. For those who cannot attend, I am asking you to please lift up your voices in prayer to our Father during that time. Let God hear the voices of His people all around the globe asking Him to wrap Mildred in His loving embrace and bring healing to her body. We are thankful for each of you.

LOIS

I was talking with my friend Lois the other night. Lois is a lady I met when I first started taking chemo, and I had not talked with her for a while. She called me, and we were finally able to catch up with each other. Lois is the only person left that I met in the chemo room when I first started. She and I are the only ones still alive. It was good to talk with her and reminisce. She is doing well and looking forward to going down to Georgia to see her mom and dad who are 90 years old. Lois is constantly going on vacations or taking trips even though she has cancer and is going through chemo

> and radiation. She still has that positive outlook. When we talk, we just laugh and have a good time. We talk about different things, even some of the things that made us sick, but we laugh about them anyway. That's the reason I said earlier that you have to keep a positive frame of mind on this journey because the more positive you are, the better you will be.

Day 1,212 PC

Glory Hallelujah

November 10, 2015

On Monday night we were blessed by so many who participated in praying for us, whether at our home or around the world. This morning Mildred and I woke up at 5:00 a.m., prepared for our trip to the hospital, and then spent time praying. We were at the hospital by 6:30 a.m., and shortly after they took Mildred back to prepare her. After more than an hour, they brought me back, and we got to spend the final 15 minutes together.

Right before they took Mildred to the operating room, her surgeon came by and asked if we were okay and still wanted to do this. We both readily replied yes. He said with a very confident attitude, "Then let's go take that gallbladder out. It was approximately 8:45 a.m. when they wheeled Mildred back to the OR. I left the surgery area and went down to the hospital chapel to pray.

At 10:00 a.m., her surgeon came down to see me, grinning from ear to ear. He knew that the least probable but most beneficial outcome had occurred. He told me that the procedure could not have gone any better. He did not encounter any problems, and the gallbladder just lifted right out. He said, "It was as if everything simply moved out of the way" so he could get the gallbladder. Mildred was in recovery and would be for a few hours before they took her up to a room. His plan is to remove the temporary tube they put in during the surgery and send her home tomorrow. At 6:00 p.m., she was sitting up in bed eating a roast pork dinner and looking as though nothing had happened.

Sometimes I feel like Peter must have felt when Jesus told him to come out of the boat and walk across the water to Him. Even though I have seen and continue to see miraculous things during our journey, the element of fear was still present during this part of the journey. Every time we encounter another bump in the road, God simply takes us over it. We have been blessed so many times. I do believe that a significant factor on our journey and blessings is the power of prayer. *Prayer really works!* We have many people throughout this country and in other parts of the world praying for us on a regular basis. The voices of God's people continue to lift us up to Him, and we thank each and every one of you. We would not be able to continue this journey if it were not for the strength each of you gives us through your prayers and other means of support. We look forward to getting back to ministering to others in the next week or so after Mildred regains her strength. Once again, *thank you.*

And thank you to our most loving God.

HIS HANDS

I had the gallbladder surgery on November 10th. The night before my surgery we had a prayer service at our house, and approximately 65 people were there. In addition, there were people all around the world praying for me. That prayer service was so wonderful and so powerful that we continue to see blessings as a result. I made it through the surgery despite the odds I was given. God had another plan. Ever since the gallbladder has been removed, I have had so much strength and energy that I keep marching and trying to help others. I have been so busy. I did not realize how much energy the gallbladder infection was robbing me of.

Day 1,214 PC

She Is Home

November 12, 2015

Mildred was released from the hospital last night. She still has a low level of pain but nothing like what she had been experiencing. She was able to sleep through the night. I expect she will continue to improve over the next few days and hopefully resume her normal activity by Monday. Again, we thank each of you for everything.

Words do not adequately convey how much each of you has touched our hearts.

Day 1,227 PC
Onward We March

November 25, 2015

Last Sunday we were able to attend church and give thanks to our Father for all He has done for us, particularly these past few weeks. On Monday, we went to see the surgeon for Mildred's post-op visit. Everything was great. While the pathology report on the gallbladder indicated that it certainly was infected and inflamed, there was no evidence of any cancer in it. The surgeon was full of smiles and asked for hugs before we left. He was definitely inspired by Mildred's presence.

This morning we visited with our oncologist. He, too, is amazed by Mildred. He said she is like the Energizer bunny—"she just keeps going and going and going." All her labs were within normal range, and she will begin receiving chemo on Monday, November 30th. The doctor plans to resume her three-week schedule of treatments and does not feel it is necessary to return to the two-week schedule. While the cancer has grown during her five-month hiatus from chemo, it is still within the lower range of her normal. Aside from the chemo, the number one priority now is for her to gain back some weight. She weighed 102 pounds this morning. Otherwise everything is fine, and her doctor remains optimistic.

As we approach tomorrow, Thanksgiving Day, Mildred and I have a great deal to be thankful for. We have been and continue to be blessed in countless ways. The reality is that every day is Thanksgiving Day for us.

Whether it is overcoming another bump in the road or simply

having God's presence with us, we are so blessed. We give thanks to each of you for your participation in our journey. We pray that God will bless you every day as He has done for us. Have a blessed Thanksgiving!

Day 1,291 PC

Continued Blessings

January 28, 2016

It has been a while since I posted anything, but rest assured, we are still on our journey. After recovering from her gallbladder surgery, Mildred began chemo treatments on Monday, November 30th. This was her first treatment since June 22nd prior to her gallbladder becoming an issue. During this time period, her CEA number, which is an indicator of the level of cancer in her, went from 37.8 to 287. As a reference point, on the day she was diagnosed in July 2012, her CEA was slightly over 400. In addition, she lost weight, coming in at 99—102 pounds.

We met with our oncologist today to review her most recent progress. She has gained some weight, now 112 pounds. More importantly, her CEA has declined to 189. In addition, since she recovered from surgery, she has had much more energy and has not had any of the significant side effects of the chemo. While she becomes fatigued during the week she receives chemo, she has not experienced the more drastic issues. In fact, she told the oncologist today, "I feel like I have as much energy as I did before I was diagnosed." She has been able to be in the salon three days a week, although she has decided not to stand behind the chair anymore.

She will focus on managing the salon, meeting, and greeting clients, working with and educating the employees, and more. Her spirit, and through her the Holy Spirit, is what truly makes the salon what it is.

Since Mildred has recovered from the surgery, we have been able to ramp our ministry back up. Aside from ministering to fellow patients in the treatment room, we have visited patients at home and in the hospital, run errands, done grocery shopping, and regularly prayed for them and with them. We were also blessed to share our testimony at our New Year's Eve church service. We are also actively praying for a dear friend of ours who was recently diagnosed with breast cancer and will have a mastectomy on Monday, February 8th. We pray that our Father will give her and her family the strength to overcome the surgery and that He will let them know He is walking right beside them, just as He has done for us.

In summary, Mildred and I continue to be so blessed by our Father on this journey. We give Him thanks and praise for all He has done and continues to do, and we eagerly anticipate the future He has in store for us.

Holy, holy, holy, Lord God Almighty!

Day 1,310 PC

A Vision and a Calling

February 16, 2016

Most who know Mildred are aware that she is at a spiritual level that most of us aspire to be. By far her dominant spiritual gift is the gift of prophecy. She has an ability to communicate with and receive communication from our Father that very few Christians have. One night this past December while she was asleep, she received a vision from our Father. Her vision had her standing in front of a group of women and children in what she described as a crater-like ancient ruins sort of amphitheater in the country of Jordan where she was sharing the story of her journey. When she awoke, she shared her vision with me. Neither of us has ever been to Jordan or the Middle East, so we were not sure what the purpose of the vision was.

About three weeks later on Sunday, January 3rd, we went to church. When we arrived, we looked at our church bulletin, and on the outside cover an announcement said, "Seeking medical and non-medical people and professional hair stylists to minister the love of Jesus to Iraqi and Syrian refugees in Jordan." We looked at each other in amazement but with understanding, for we have experienced things like this before on our journey.

Since that Sunday, we have attended meetings, been in prayer, and asked others to pray for us as we seek our Father's will. We believe God has made his desire clear—we are to go to Jordan and minister His love to these people who have suffered so much. One of the things we have learned is that approximately 80 percent of the refugees are women and children since most of the men are either dead or involved in the fighting. While the members of the mission team and their individual roles are still being formulated, and while we still have a couple minor details to take care of, we will soon be headed to Jordan.

We will depart on Thursday, May 19th for Amman and then head to the northern part of Jordan to set up facilities and minister to the Syrian refugees for three days. After that, we will head to the southern part of Jordan to minister to the Iraqi refugees. On the last two days of the trip, we will have the opportunity to visit some of the sites often referenced in the Bible during Christ's time on this earth. While we understand we may be putting ourselves in harm's way, we know our Father will keep us safe and in His embrace, no matter what.

Between now and then, we and our team have numerous tasks to complete. While preparing for this trip, we covet your prayers that our Father will strengthen Mildred and guide us in our preparations. When we leave, we ask that each of you keep us and the team in your prayers every day as we seek to do our Father's will. We are eagerly awaiting our departure and look forward to being truly on the mission field.

Day 1,317 PC

Preparations

February 23, 2016

Mildred had her labs and received chemo yesterday. Her labs were all normal, her CEA had declined slightly, and her weight was 115 pounds, down slightly from 119 but still better than it had been.

We continue to prepare for our mission to Jordan. Our team is compiling an inventory of medical supply needs, and we hope to begin procuring these items shortly. In addition, we are still in the process of attracting other medical and hair stylist personnel to our team.

We also seek your continued prayers that our Father will guide and bless our trip preparations and ultimately our mission when the time comes. We have been told by our Jordanian partners on the ground in Jordan to expect 700 to 1,000 refugees. We look forward to serving their needs and sharing God's love with them.

We continue to minister to other cancer patients. We particularly ask that you pray for Pam and Cecil. We have been ministering to Cecil for approximately a year now as he deals with his prostate cancer. The tumors continue to grow and are preventing any surgery. Pam has been in and out of the hospital these last six months battling cervical cancer and is currently hospitalized. She has been told by both her oncologist here locally as well as a second team in Houston, Texas, that there is nothing more they can do for her. We ask that you lift this brother and sister up to our Father in prayer. Pray that He will work a miracle in them as He has done with Mildred. Pray that He will comfort them, shower them with His love, and bring them healing. Nothing is impossible where He is concerned.

PAM

I met another woman recently who attends our church. Her name is Pam. She has cervical cancer and is having a difficult time. She was receiving chemo locally, but the chemo was not effective. She then went to one of the large cancer centers in Texas, but they told her there was nothing else they could do. Pam came back home, and I talked to her last week. We had planned to meet at her house, but when I went there, she was not at home. I called and left a message on her cell phone, but I did not know what was happening. I hope I will be able to talk with her in the next few days. Her friend called me a few days later to tell me that Pam had been called home. She only lived a little over six months from the time she was diagnosed, a little over three weeks after going to Texas to visit the cancer center there. I had been able to visit with her several times, and I was glad to have had that time with her. She was a great believer, and she was not afraid to be called home. I was glad for her.

Day 1,322 PC

Another Bump

February 28, 2016

Saturday morning, Mildred awoke with pain in the entire length of her left leg. Throughout the day, the pain increased. Finally, the pain reached such a severe level that I took her to the Princess Anne Hospital ER at 4:30 on Sunday morning. They took X-rays, did blood work, and took ultrasounds of both her legs. The only negative symptom they found was that her white blood count was significantly elevated. As a result, they admitted her to the hospital. Since that time, they have been running a variety of tests and have found no infection or a reason for the pain. Her blood pressure continues to be elevated, so they are giving her medicine to lower it. Around 4:00 p.m., they put her on a pain pump. Mildred is able to handle a significant level of pain, but this pain is so severe that she is in tears when she is awake. The hope is that she will sleep most of the night since she had little sleep last night. She is now receiving a constant dose of significant pain medicine. They have discussed performing CT and bone scans tomorrow morning, but nothing is definite. The primary focus right now is to try to get the pain down to a manageable level.

I am asking each of you to pray that our Father will impart medical wisdom to the medical staff and that He will heal her from the pain. Mildred and I know He still has this and will continue to walk with us. While this is a painful bump, it is still just a bump. God has called us to go to Jordan, and He will not allow this to get in the way. Father, I pray that you will remove this pain from your angel daughter's body, that you will heal her as you have done throughout this journey so we can continue to serve you. We praise your holy name!

Day 1,323 PC

Improvement

February 29, 2016

Mildred had a rough night last night. They still have not been able to determine the exact cause of her leg pain. Every test and scan have come back negative other than her white blood count. No abnormalities have been noted in any part of her leg. The hospital doctors and her oncologist are mystified as to what is causing her pain. They are ruling things out but have not been able to determine a specific cause.

While I cannot say with medical certainty that her white count is the cause of all this, there certainly does appear to be some degree of correlation between the two. We will see what tomorrow brings—one day at a time with our Father beside us giving us the strength to face and overcome whatever lies ahead. We thank each of you for all your prayers and love.

Day 1,324 PC
Continued Improvement

March 1, 2016

Even though the medical staff still has not been able to determine a cause for her pain, all of Mildred's numbers are heading in the right direction. She was able to walk using a walker. They took her completely off the IV and started giving her pill antibiotics to fight any infection that may be present in her body.

Our Father continues to wrap Mildred in His loving embrace. This afternoon we were visited by three members of a group called the Healing Touch Ministry. They laid hands on her and prayed over her for about 10 minutes, much like we do when we attend soaking prayer at our church. We were able to feel His presence in the room as it brought total peace and tranquility to us. We just continue to be blessed in so many ways by so many people on behalf of our Father. We thank and praise Him for all He has done and continues to do for us.

Day 1,325 PC
Back Home

March 2, 2016

Mildred was able to come home this afternoon. Her white count is still slightly elevated compared to normal but continuing to decrease. Her blood pressure is normal, and she no longer feels any pain in her left leg. She is a little tired but continuing to improve. The doctors still were not able to determine a specific cause, but we are all in agreement that the correlation between the white count and the pain cannot be ignored. We probably will never know for sure. We will continue to move forward one day at a time as we have all along on our journey. We take each day as it comes and make the best of it as we walk alongside our Father who never leaves us.

Day 1,330 PC
A Few Minutes of Fear

March 7, 2016

Mildred was discharged from the hospital this past Wednesday. Prior to being discharged, she had developed a slight chest cough indicative of bronchitis. The doctors felt that she could take the antibiotics and steroids they had prescribed and rest at home. However, over the next few days, her fatigue level and coughing frequency gradually increased. On Sunday morning after resting for a few hours, she wanted to take a shower. In the shower, she had a respiratory attack and could not breathe. The harder she tried to get air into her lungs, the more difficult it was, and she began to panic. I tried to focus on calming her down and prevent her from going into shock, but it was obvious to me that we needed help. I called 911, and the EMTs were dispatched. Before they arrived, she continued to fight for breath, and I tried to calm her. During those few minutes, I felt helpless. The only thing I could do besides try to calm her was pray that our Father would give her air to breathe. The EMTs arrived, stabilized her, assessed her, put her on oxygen, and transported her by ambulance to the ER.

When we arrived, they kept her on oxygen, but her breathing was very labored and her heart rate was high. After doing blood work and a chest X-ray, they began giving her breathing treatments and an IV to hydrate her. They did an EKG and then a contrast CT scan. The sum of everything is that she has pneumonia in both lungs in addition to a pulmonary embolism (blood clot) in her right lung. They began treating her with a combination of steroids, blood thinners, high-powered antibiotics, and another drug to lower her anxiety and heart rate. Late Sunday evening, they moved her to a room and continued to "pound" her all night with various meds. She is weak from the physical and mental strain but was able to get some rest overnight.

I had the opportunity to speak with her attending physician this morning. Mildred's numbers have improved slightly compared to when she first came in. However, the doctor is concerned about her heart rate still being elevated and possible reductions of her kidney functions. She said we were fortunate that Mildred did not die on Sunday. The bottom line is that she is improving but still has significant issues to overcome.

Mildred and I talked and prayed tonight, and we are both of the same belief. Not only has God had this entire journey, but He has also called us to go to Jordan. We know He will heal her so we will be able to answer His call and complete the mission He has given us. May His power and glory continue to be evidenced by His loving angel daughter.

This past week has been one of our difficult times, not only with Mildred's condition but also with the homegoing of Pam, who passed away Thursday evening, and the difficulties and extreme pain Cecil is experiencing. They are going to do some radiation on his tumors today and then give him chemo on Tuesday, with the hope that they can at least decrease the size of the tumors and allow him to undergo surgery. One thing you learn on the cancer and faith journeys is that no matter what happens today, no matter how wonderful today may be, there will be bumps in the road as you go forward. We pray that our Father will give Cecil and Mildred healing and strength as they both continue their journeys. We pray that He will impart medical wisdom to the professionals caring for them. Most of all, we pray that He will continue to embrace them in His loving arms and give them His peace. Please pray for both of them today.

Day 1,331 PC

More Improvement

March 8, 2016

Mildred is improving today. Her numbers were all in the normal ranges, but she is still coughing and hacking. They are continuing to give her antibiotics and steroids to combat the pneumonia, and she is still receiving blood thinner injections. She is weaker than normal but no longer in the state of exhaustion she was in on Sunday and Monday.

She was able to receive visitors today and would welcome anyone who wants to see her. Please also know that when you visit her, be it at home or in the hospital, when you send a message to let us know you are praying for us, or when you bring meals and such, you are infusing us with our Father's strength. Doing these things lets us know you are not simply standing on the sidelines watching us on our journey but are down in the mud with us engaged in the battle. We know that however long we remain on this journey, we will continue to encounter bumps in the road as the enemy tries to stop us. Let him take his best shot because we know it is not just us on this journey but rather, we are marching with our Father's army. There are countless fellow soldiers marching with us and our Father, and we continue to draw our strength from each of you. We will *not* be defeated so long as we have each of you in the fight with us.

Day 1,333 PC
Another Bump Overcome

March 10, 2016

Mildred's white count today was a statistically insignificant difference from her count on Wednesday. Based upon her count remaining stable and the lessening of pain in her left leg, she was able to come home late this afternoon. She is resting in her recliner and catching up on her mail. She still has a small amount of coughing and hacking but is significantly better than she was this past Sunday. She will remain on a blood thinner for a minimum of the next three weeks. After that, her oncologist, who we are scheduled to see for labs on Tuesday and consultation on Thursday, will make the call as to whether or not she should stay on the blood thinner. My thought is that he will keep her on it at least until we return from Jordan at the end of May. We will know more next week. Once again, our Father and His army have helped us overcome another bump in the road. We just keep marching!

Day 1,364 PC

A Sad Day

April 10, 2016

Yesterday afternoon, Mildred and I were told of the death of a very dear and longtime friend, Nancy. She was like a sister to Mildred and a friend to me. Nancy would call and check on Mildred every two to three days. I became very used to hearing, "I'm just checking in to see how you are doing." They and another friend would gather the first Monday of each month to eat and play cards together at Nancy's house. Nancy would take Mildred to appointments when I was not able to do so. Nancy came to the salon every Wednesday morning to have her hair done. In warmer months, Mildred, Nancy, and Mildred's sister Marie went fishing. Nancy was the embodiment of what a true friend is all about.

She was a very intelligent woman as well as a talented artist who at various times had her own studio in Paris and New York City. While we did not agree on every issue, I always enjoyed discussing them with her. She was a "dying breed" in our world today. She was someone you could disagree with and yet gain better understanding from. She could disagree with you but never be disagreeable to you.

While Mildred and I know that Nancy, through her own faith, now resides with our Father, the pain of loss still hurts. She was such a regular, day-to-day part of our lives. She was what so many of us hope to have but rarely do—a true friend. We will miss her terribly, and we thank our Father for bringing her into our lives.

Day 1,385 PC
The Preparations Are Underway

May 1, 2016

As you know, Mildred and I have committed to being part of a mission team heading to Jordan to minister to Syrian (predominantly Muslim) and Iraqi (predominantly Christian) refugees. The team's efforts will include medical and haircutting services but most importantly will be delivering our Father's love to these people who have lost and suffered so much. We will have the opportunity to minister to primarily women and children in group and individual settings. Our team has been planning the details of this effort for the past few months, and our departure date of May 19th is rapidly approaching. We have been so blessed to receive both financial and prayer support from so many people. We especially ask for your prayers during this month of May as we both prepare and then implement our Father's plan. We are so eager to see what He has in store for us in Jordan and how we will be able to impact people's lives.

During these past couple months, upon learning of our trip, people have usually asked two questions:

1. Are you not afraid to be going to such a volatile place where so much conflict and unrest exist?

2. Will Mildred be healthy and strong enough to handle the physical rigors of the mission?

The answer to the first question is *no, we are not afraid.* While we understand that we will be as close as 30 kilometers from the Syrian border at one point, we know our Father has called us through the vision He gave Mildred. He has a definite reason for us to be in Jordan, and we know He will keep us in His loving embrace. We truly have the *"peace that passes all understanding"* and await with eager anticipation the opportunity to serve.

The answer to the second question is part faith and part medical science, We discussed this trip with our doctors prior to committing to go, and all of them felt that as long as all her indicators were where they needed to be prior to leaving, she should be okay. Since she was discharged from the hospital a couple months ago, all her vital signs and lab work have been right where they are supposed to be. Her weight has been stable in the 115—120 pound range, her blood work has been within normal ranges, and she has been able to receive her chemo on schedule. In fact, she is scheduled to receive her next chemo treatment tomorrow morning. That will be the last treatment before we depart, and she will have more than two weeks to recover from it. We also both received our necessary vaccinations the week before last.

During the last month or so, her physical energy level has been strong enough that she has been able to regularly do normal things.

She has been to the salon two or three days a week. She and the girls went to Richmond for two days to attend a hair show. She has been planting annual plants in various parts of our yard. We believed from the time we were called that God would give her body, mind, and soul the energy and strength to answer this call. He has done that, and we know He will continue to do that. Yes, we will have to ensure that she paces herself and does not overdo it, but we have no doubt that she will be able to be a tremendous blessing to those she meets in Jordan.

We thank each of you for your continued prayers and love. We anxiously await the opportunity to share with you the details of our ministry efforts in Jordan once we return.

Day 1,400 PC

Departure Is Imminent

May 16, 2016

In approximately 60 hours, our mission team will begin traveling to Jordan. On Thursday morning, we will meet at the church and begin the drive to Dulles Airport in Washington, DC. We will depart at 9:35 p.m. on an 8.5 hour flight to Paris. We will lay over there approximately 2.5 hours and then fly 4.5 hours to Amman, which is 7 hours ahead of the United States, and then land in Amman at 8:20 p.m. on Friday evening.

We spent this afternoon and evening organizing all our supplies and packing them for the flight. In addition, we reviewed all the detailed plans we have been working on these past few months to ensure everyone understands their roles and the various details associated with our mission. Most importantly, we had a time of commissioning and prayer this evening. Individuals who have made this trip in the past two years, family members, and some church elders came to pray with us and for us, and lay hands on us. We seek our Father's guidance, wisdom, and love as we prepare to go forth in His service. Hearing members of previous years' teams talk about how the trip impacted their lives and how their team was able to impact the lives they came in contact with was an emotional experience. We pray that our team will have the same or even greater impact on those we meet and minister to.

Tomorrow evening, our life group members will meet at our house for another evening of prayer with us and for us. We will be seeking our Father's guidance, wisdom, and love not only tomorrow evening but every day between now and the time of our return. Mildred and I ask each of you to pray at least once a day between now and May 31st when we return for our team and our mission. Pray that we will be able to show God's love, His healing, and His joy. Pray that He will keep each of us safe from harm. Pray that we will be able to bring understanding of the one true God to the Muslims we meet through His words and our actions. Pray that when we return, we will be able to hear His words—*Well done, good and faithful servant.*

Day 1,406 PC
Jordan Day 4

May 22, 2016

We arrived in Jordan on Friday night at 8:10 p.m. Jordan time (1:10 a.m. EDT) after leaving home at 11:00 a.m. on Thursday. Needless to say, we were all tired and sleep-deprived. After getting some sleep, we spent Saturday doing orientation and a walk-through with one of our Jordanian partners, as well as unpacking. It also was the first time the entire team was together in one place, so we had time to get to know each other. We left Amman at 7:00 a.m. on Sunday and drove to Irbid, a town 30 kilometers from the Syrian border, where we met our other Jordanian partner and finished the setup to begin seeing patients. At 10:00 a.m., we began seeing patients who were already lined up and waiting for us when we first arrived. Over the course of the day, we saw 153 patients (mom+children=1 patient). We were able to provide general medicine, internal medicine, eye services with free glasses, dietician services, personal counseling, pediatric medicine, and free pharmacy services, as well as haircutting and styling.

The overwhelming number of patients were women and children with conditions ranging from colds and flu to a three-year-old Syrian girl who had a hole in her heart. Because her family fled Syria and they are not considered residents of Jordan, they cannot receive medical services without paying in full. Needless to say, they have nothing and have not found work. Please pray for this family that our Father would open a door for them to be saved, both spiritually and physically.

After a long day, we returned to our living quarters for showers and dinner. After eating and reviewing the events of the day and discussing how we can improve our procedures to see more patients, we retired for the night. We will be up early tomorrow and begin seeing patients at 9:00 a.m. I feel like words are inadequate to describe the broken families and difficult living conditions we witnessed today. One of our patients talked about how afraid they are when, even now that they are in Jordan, they can still occasionally hear the sounds of the mortar explosions just across the border in Syria. We pray that our Father will end these conflicts and enable families to return to some form of normalcy. We pray that He will embrace them with His love and bring them peace.

Day 1,407 PC
Jordan Day 5

May 23, 2016

Today we were still in Irbid and saw 158 patients, again with the overwhelming majority being mothers and children. On the bus ride back to our quarters at the end of the day, one of our female doctors shared an event she had experienced that day. After she finished treating a Muslim woman who was dressed in full-length dress and hijab, the woman, with tears in her eyes, hugged the doctor's neck and thanked her. She thanked the doctor for taking care of her, but more importantly, she thanked the doctor for treating her with humanity and respect. She went on to tell the doctor that everyone looks and treats her and her family, Syrian refugees, as worthless.

She was so thankful that an American Christian doctor did not do that.

That is why we are here. The actions of a small team of Christians reflecting our Father's love can do so much more than any words we could ever say. If we are able to change the hearts and minds of a few, perhaps many more will follow. May our Father be glorified in all we do.

Day 1,410 PC

Jordan Day 8

May 26, 2016

The last few days have been eventful to say the least. Tuesday was our last day in Irbid, and we saw about 150 patients. Our experiences were very similar to the first two days, and we continued to experience the same kind of love. Tuesday night we drove back to Amman to begin the next three days there. We would see 180 patients, not as many children as we had seen during our days in Irbid. We still experienced the joy and thanks from many of them.

But on Wednesday morning, our troubles began. One of our team members awoke with severe stomach pain, fever, and vomiting. Wednesday night and Thursday morning, it was my turn to be on the sick list with a sinus infection and fever. Then Thursday afternoon, our Jordanian hosts brought Mildred back to our quarters because she was experiencing diarrhea. They made us both a large bowl of chicken soup, and we have been nursing it ever since. We both hope to be able to leave on Friday.

The hardest part about mission trips is saying goodbye. You

spend a week plus serving with people on your team and the local people you meet and then you have to say goodbye. Tomorrow we will say goodbye to our Amman partners just as we did on Tuesday to our Irbid partners. We have served about 1,000 patients over the six days of clinic, and hopefully we have made a difference in their lives. We thank each of you for your support and prayers. Mildred and I ask that you lift us both up in prayer so we will be able to serve tomorrow, our last day.

Day 1,411 PC
Jordan Day 9

May 27, 2016

Today we finished the last day of clinics. We saw 234 patients, and tonight we are scheduled to have dinner at our Amman host's home. Mildred stayed home and rested. She improved some but spent the day in bed and was able to eat chicken soup. She hopes to be well enough to do the next two days of tourist events, but we will see how she is in the morning. Please pray for all three of us who have battled sickness. Also please pray that the unrest currently happening in Paris will calm down. We have team members who are scheduled to fly to Paris later this evening, spend the day there tomorrow, and then fly home. In addition, every team member is scheduled to fly to Paris to connect with their flight home between tonight and Monday evening. We pray for the safety of our team members and for everyone's safe passage home.

Day 1,414 PC
Jordan Day 12

May 30, 2016

We were originally scheduled to do two days of tourist activities, but we decided to let Mildred rest instead. We were able to sleep until later in the afternoon. We had lunch and dinner with the founder of our Amman partner, her parents, and in-laws. It was a very enjoyable and moving experience. Her father-in-law is a retired general from the Jordanian army but has served as a Christian pastor for many years. At the end of our time together, he asked everyone if they would lay hands on Mildred while he anointed her with oil and prayed over this "special woman of God who had come to bless Jordan and her people." He delivered a powerful prayer.

On Sunday, we took a car ride to visit a few sites. The first site we visited was Mount Nebo. We had the opportunity to stand where Moses stood when he viewed the Promised Land so many years ago. We could see the Jordan River and where it reached the Dead Sea. We saw the entire valley as it traversed to the West Bank of Israel. In addition, somewhere within our view was where the body of Moses was buried. Think about the enormity of that. We were standing and viewing things that are written in the Bible. What an awesome experience that was! Upon leaving Mount Nebo, we went to Madaba, a town 8 kilometers away. Madaba is famous for its churches with mosaic tile artwork, including St. George Greek Orthodox Church that was built over the remains of a Byzantine church that contains the oldest known map of the Holy Land. The map is contained within the floor of the church and is constructed of original mosaic tiles dating back to the 1300s. After eating lunch, we traveled to the shore of the Dead Sea and had the opportunity to see that people really do float in this body of salt water. Again, it was just an incredible feeling to be reliving history.

Today (Monday) we traveled to the town of Jerash, a modem-day city adjacent to the remaining ruins of its ancient Roman counterpart by the same name. The ruins are approximately 6 square miles and have significant remnants of the original Roman town. There are cobblestone streets with marketplace stalls, open pavilions, living areas, numerous stone columns, and two absolutely stunning areas.

The first area was an arena where the Romans held chariot races in much the same fashion as I recall seeing Charlton Heston portray it in the movies. There were horse stalls for the horses that led out into an open arena with center posts that defined the circular track. There were viewing stands, some of them box seating for royalty, that were approximately 20 rows up. You could just feel the experiences that occurred in this arena.

The second area sent chills down my back. We walked out onto the ground level of an outdoor amphitheater, the one in Mildred's vision. As we stood in the center, we could see for 180 degrees the rows of stone seats that rose for approximately 30 rows. When we turned around, we saw a raised platform with seats for royalty and politicians. From this platform, they could speak to the crowd and have discussions and debates. If we talked at ground level, we could hear our voices resonate off the ruins.

I cannot begin to adequately describe what we were able to see and experience, let alone the fact that this matched what Mildred saw in her vision. As we walk around, we could feel the lifeblood of the ancient Romans who once inhabited this place. Tonight we will conclude our time here in Jordan and return home. What an awesome experience it has been.

Day 1,417 PC
Jordan Day 15

June 2, 2016

We left our living quarters at 10:00 p.m. Jordan time, and 27 hours later, without regard to time zone changes, we touched down at Norfolk International Airport in Virginia. Needless to say, it was a long, tiring journey home and lacked the excitement of our time in Jordan. We have spent the last two days recovering, unpacking, doing laundry, and gradually getting back to our normal lifestyle.

While we are glad to be home, we are also sad that the journey is over. It was simply an incredibly awesome collection of experiences. We were blessed to have a very talented team where each person performed their individual roles to the absolute best of their abilities. The focus was completely on serving the people we came to serve, and everyone was willing to do whatever needed to be done at any point in time to accomplish our fundamental mission.

We were able to serve the medical needs of 1,050 people through the services of a dentist, ophthalmologist, dietician, pediatrician, internal medicine doctor, ER doctor, two Jordanian general medicine doctors for a couple days, and a professional nursing staff to support all the doctors. We provided over $25,000 worth of prescription medicines at no charge to the patients we saw. We ministered to the children through arts and crafts, games, football (soccer), coloring, and more. Mildred was able to serve 92 clients. A significant number of the clients asked to take her photo with them because they wanted to be able to always remember this lovely woman who helped them feel beautiful again. Most importantly, we displayed the love of our Father to both the Syrian and Iraqi populations in many ways. We repeatedly received thanks and love from the people we saw.

Every member of our mission team said they were willing to do this again. We hope our Father will use our experiences to attract others to our team. Informally we have set a goal of 30 team members next year. Compared to the 19 we had this year, that would allow us to serve even more people and make a greater difference. The trip was truly a lifetime-remembering event that will stay with us for the rest of our lives. We are motivated to return again. Our hope and prayer, however, is that our efforts will not be necessary because the conflicts in the Middle East will be resolved. If not, we look forward to being able to serve our Father and His people once again.

We thank each of you for your continued support and prayers that enabled this trip to occur. We could not have done it without each of you.

Day 1,467 PC

We Have Had a Good Run

July 22, 2016

During these last few months, we have been extremely blessed. Mildred has been in good health with good energy levels and no significant issues to contend with. The Jordan trip was a memorable event, and we received many more blessings than those we were able to give. Actually, over these last four years, we have been blessed far more than any blessings we have given. I remember the surgeon's post-op words to me four years ago on July 17, 2012. "Get her affairs in order; she will be lucky to live two years." Sitting here today, I could have never envisioned the many blessings, events, and people we have been so fortunate to have in our lives. If the journey were to end tonight, I would be very thankful for all Mildred and I have experienced these last four years, and I would celebrate her homecoming with our Father.

These thoughts are particularly relevant this evening as we have encountered another large bump in the road. Since returning from Jordan, Mildred has had three chemo treatments with accompanying labs. The first set of labs showed a CEA of 260, an increase from 180 prior to the trip. The next set of labs showed that the CEA had declined to 179. This past Monday, we were told that her latest CEA has increased significantly to 304. To put these numbers in perspective, her CEA on July 17, 2012, was slightly above 400.

Mildred received her third chemo treatment this past Monday but it has been a rocky few days since. She experienced two days of constipation that had to be relieved with laxative pills. Her system then immediately went the other way, and she began experiencing frequent diarrhea Wednesday evening. That has continued through today. The result is that she has become severely dehydrated and fatigued. As a result, I took her to the oncologist's office to receive an infusion of fluids. She will receive more fluids on Saturday and Sunday as well. She has lost 6 pounds since this past Monday. It is the first time in a number of months that she has experienced the full range of side effects from the chemo.

The result of this is that her body may not be able to withstand the impact of chemo more frequently than every three weeks. The oncologist would like to put her back on a two-week schedule to try to overpower the cancer cells that have produced the high CEA level. However, given the events of this week so far and the effect the drugs have had on her, we agree that we will have to wait and see what happens in the next few days. She needs to have at least one week of normalcy and stability in her body to be able to receive chemo. If that week does not occur until the third week after receiving chemo, the cancer may grow faster than her current chemo drugs can overcome.

Throughout this journey, our Father has either walked by our side or, in fact, carried us. This is one of those times where we are relying on His strength to be imparted into Mildred's body and into both of our spirits. We pray that He will cover her with His healing hands and give her body the strength it needs to overcome the chemo's side effects. We pray that His healing hands will once again make her cancer-free. We ask each of you and her extensive prayer warrior network to lift her up to Him. Pray that He will rain down His love upon her, heal her, and give her body strength.

Day 1,473 PC

Onward We Go

July 28, 2016

This past week has been the typical roller coaster ride on our journey. From last Wednesday through Saturday, the side effects of the chemo were kicking Mildred hard. On Sunday, she began to feel better and had her third consecutive day of fluids. However, on Monday, she went backward, experiencing more severe diarrhea, fatigue, and vomiting. Then on Tuesday, she awoke and felt more normal than she had in over a week. Yesterday, she was even better, but she had dental surgery in the afternoon.

Today, we went to the oncologist's office for labs and vitals. All her blood work was within normal ranges. Her blood pressure was slightly elevated (130/90) but not a significant concern. The medical opinion was that she should be okay to receive chemo this Monday and return to a two-week schedule. We will not know what her latest CEA is until Monday but we continue to pray that it will have begun to decline. The medical focus is to get the CEA back down under 100 by using more frequent and, if necessary, stronger chemo meds. The key is whether her body can withstand the impact.

We thank each of you for your continued prayers. We ask our Father to give her strength and healing so we can continue to minister to others. We had the opportunity to meet a new patient today, Phyllis, and we look forward to continuing to meet others. We know what the purpose of this journey is, and we will continue to live it every day.

Day 1,476 PC

Waiting and Praying

August 1, 2016

Mildred had an okay weekend—a little bit of fatigue and a sore mouth from the dental surgery, but no significant side effects from the chemo. We were able to attend church yesterday for the kickoff of our church's annual month of prayer. Mildred is now back to an every two-week chemo schedule. Her weight is down 2 pounds to 110, but her labs and blood pressure are in the normal ranges. Her latest CEA from the labs that were done last week is 275, a slight improvement from the previous 300.

Last year, the older of my two stepbrothers, who is my same age, found out he has multiple myeloma—bone cancer. I have only seen John four or five times in the last 45 years since we have lived totally different lives. He has lived most of his life in South Philadelphia. I left there in 1968 when my father died. Last week his oncologist said there was nothing more they could do for him. The cancer in his bones has advanced throughout his entire body. It has infected his brain, liver, and lungs. They sent him home yesterday with hospice care and gave him two weeks at the most to live.

He has been and continues to be in significant pain. My younger stepbrother, Joe, told me last night that John's face and skin are sagging and pulling away from the bones as they deteriorate. He has lesions throughout his body that are continuing to expand. He is receiving morphine, and hospice will continue to increase the strength and frequency over the next few days until John passes. He will die an excruciating death. My stepsister Rose has been with John for the last couple days and will remain until everything is over. Joe and Angela (my stepsister) will both arrive in Philadelphia on Tuesday. Rose is a fervent Christian, and when John is awake, she talks with him about Christ and salvation. My heart aches for John, knowing the horribly painful death he will experience and that he may not truly know Christ as his Lord and Savior. I will be praying fervently until John passes that he will come to accept Jesus as his Savior and that our Father will not let him linger in pain too long. I ask each of you to lift him up in prayer that he will accept Christ as his Savior. As long as he has breath, it is not too late. May our Father have mercy on him.

Day 1,481 PC

A Soul Departs

August 6, 2016

On Friday morning at 6:45 a.m., my stepbrother John passed away. The cancer ravaged his body in the end. His pain was unimaginable. Hospice had to double the normal morphine dose they give patients at the end to try to reduce the pain. His body fought, but in the end he succumbed. Prior to passing, he received the last rites from a Catholic priest who prayed over him. Only John and our Father know whether he accepted Christ as his Savior. I pray that he did.

John was diagnosed with his cancer approximately eight months before he died. With the exception of two people, everyone we have met prior to these last few months have died from their cancers. I continue to be so thankful to our Father that we are now more than four years on our cancer journey. Clearly, I have no idea when our journey will end, but we will keep marching and ministering until it does. We will continue to make every day count. Tell your spouse you love them. Thank someone for something they may have done for you. Do something for someone you may not even know. When your head hits the pillow each night, say at least one positive thing you have experienced that day—something that made the day important. May our Father bless each of you.

Day 1,489 PC

The Difficult and the Good

August 14, 2016

Mildred is still on an every two-week chemo schedule. She received her most recent chemo on Monday, August 1st. Since that time, the chemo has literally kicked the crap out of her. On Wednesday and for the 11 days since, she has had diarrhea constantly. She has been to the oncologist five days to receive IV fluids to keep her hydrated. Her weight has declined to 107 pounds, a decrease of 10 pounds since we returned from Jordan. She has been on two different anti-diarrhea medicines, and neither of them has stopped the diarrhea. The chemo she was scheduled to receive tomorrow has been rescheduled for Wednesday, August 17th. If she is still experiencing diarrhea tomorrow, we will need to return to the oncologist for another bag of fluids and further evaluation.

The good news is that her CEA has declined to 215, a decrease of 89 points from her most recent high of 304. Someone at the oncologist's office on Friday asked why we don't take some time off from chemo and go have some quality of life play time. The answer is that is *not* where God has led us. You see, He has given us quality of life throughout this journey. We were able to attend church this morning, and He spoke volumes to us through the message, "Unanswered Prayer."

> *I was given a thorn in my flesh, a messenger of Satan, to torment me. Three times I pleaded with the Lord to take it away from me. But he said to me, "My grace is sufficient for you, for my power is made perfect in weakness." Therefore I will boast all the more*

THE DIFFICULT AND THE GOOD

gladly about my weaknesses, so that Christ's power may rest on me. That is why, for Christ's sake, I delight in weaknesses, in insults, in hardships, in persecutions, in difficulties. For when I am weak, then I am strong.

—2 Cor. 12:7-10 (NIV)

Imagine the past four years if God had immediately answered our prayers for Mildred's complete healing. There would be no Voices of Hope. All the cancer patients and their caregivers we have been privileged to know and minister to would not have come into our lives. The army of prayer warriors who have mobilized to pray continuously for us would not exist. There would not have been a Jordan mission trip. I would not have had the opportunity to work in Mildred's salon and meet all the clients and employees I have been blessed to come to know. Most importantly, I would still be the person I was instead of the person I have become.

Has our Father failed to answer any of our prayers? Absolutely not. He answers all our prayers for strength each and every day. He embraces us in His love and lets us know He is still walking alongside us. Some days, He picks us up and carries us. He brings more people into our lives who need our love and service. In His infinite wisdom, He has answered the prayers that are in our best interest. However, the prayers for complete and final healing remain unanswered today. Cancer remains the thorn in Mildred's side. We still have much to be done, and our journey is not yet complete. I have *no doubt* that God will answer those prayers, whether it is 20 days from now or 20 years. Mildred will receive a final and complete healing. Until then, we keep marching and praying, knowing that He will eventually answer our prayer.

Day 1,536 PC
A Plateau Is Reached

September 30, 2016

Since early August, Mildred has been receiving her chemo every two weeks. During that time, she has had six CEA readings, and all of them have been in the range of 199 to 215. The differences in the readings are considered statistically insignificant. She had her latest PET scan this past Saturday. It, too, shows no significant change since her previous scan last year. Thus, her cancer has reached a plateau—it has not significantly increased or decreased.

We met with her oncologist yesterday to discuss where we are and what the next steps should be. The consensus is that as long as she remains where she is, she will go back to receiving treatment every three weeks instead of two. The impact of the two-week treatment schedule has been intense, and it has taken her body longer to recover from the effects. We will continue to take CEA readings with each treatment, and if they begin to increase, we will have to revisit the three-versus-two-week decision. The present moment feels like a resting place before the next significant phase of our journey. What our immediate future will be remains in God's hands. We will march forward and carry out whatever He tasks us with. We have complete *faith* that our journey has more to go. He will reveal things in His *time* and *place*.

> **CECIL**
>
> Cecil and Barbara, one of the couples we have been working with, have not been doing too well. He is receiving chemo but is having severe pain in his abdomen. He continues to have difficulty caring for his wife who has severe dementia. Cecil and Barbara served approximately 15 years as missionaries in Fiji. Bob and I went by to visit them yesterday, and they were very glad to see us. We did not know just how bad their circumstances were. Cecil is trying to do everything he can for his wife, as well as deal with the side effects of the chemo and the severe pain of the cancer. Bob and I were glad to help them by going to the grocery store to get food and the pharmacy to pick up his medicine. I told Cecil I would keep in touch with him to see if there was anything else we could help them with. Unfortunately, we never heard from him again. We called him numerous times on his phone but never received any response to our voicemails. We can only conclude that He was called home by our Heavenly Father.

Day 1,569 PC

A Freak

November 2, 2016

Today we had our monthly meeting with Mildred's oncologist. Her CEA was 192; her lab results were all within normal ranges; and she does need to gain some weight since she is currently at 106 pounds. Her next chemo treatment will be four weeks out instead of three.

During our conversation, Dr. Lee called her a "freak." He went on to say that based on his experience, a majority of the patients who are diagnosed at the level she was at her initial diagnosis live two years or less. Approximately 10 percent of patients live as long as she has. A significant portion of the 10 percent, while alive, live less than normal lives as they suffer the effects of treatment and the disease. Given Mildred's current physical and mental conditions, he said she is a freak. Other than the week of chemo side effects that comes with each treatment, she is able to live a fairly normal life despite the cancer.

Of course, when Dr. Lee called her a freak, she immediately responded with how blessed she has been. She stated that her Heavenly Father is responsible for her physical and spiritual condition, and it is her faith that has empowered her to this point. Dr. Lee, while stating that the chemo and medical personnel have played a part in her progress as well, agreed. "Whatever it is, I wish I could bottle it and give it to my other patients." The truth is that he can. While it does not come in a bottle, it is available to anyone who seeks God. I cannot imagine what the last four years would have been like if we did not have our Father and each of you to support us. People are still praying for us and continue to put our names on their churches' prayer lists.

Mildred is not a freak. She is just a *Christian*.

THE MINISTRY CONTINUES

My sister Mary, an oncology nurse, has referred another lady and her husband to me. Her husband is sick, and she is afraid. I am going to try to help her. Her husband has Stage 4 colon cancer and has an awesome faith in God. I talked to his wife, Virginia, last night, and she is so glad that Mary gave her my number. She is beginning to recognize that fear is not with God, and she feels better talking about her fear. I am glad she can walk away from that fear. I hope and pray that we will be able to march together. I asked her about meeting her husband, and she thought that was a good idea.

We talked about getting together after Thanksgiving. I am so looking forward to that. This week I met two other couples. They are awesome people from my church. Our church recommended us to them, and they called us. It was a blessing to meet them and another couple. For each couple, it was the wife who was afraid. Each husband is at peace. One husband is worried about his wife. The other husband is worried about his children and is trying to get his wife to where she is not afraid. That is why they came to see us. So I look forward to working with them because both couples are just awesome people.

Day 1,597 PC
So Much to Be Thankful For

November 30, 2016

The past four weeks have been filled with many blessings. We have begun ministering to two new cancer patients—Mike and Charles—and their caregivers. They are both married and have children, and both of them have Stage 4 cancer. Mike has renal (kidney) cancer, and Charles has pancreatic cancer. Both are confident in our Lord's healing, but their wives remain fearful. We have been able to share our experiences with them and will continue to uplift and encourage them.

This past week, Mildred's sister and brother-in-law flew in from Portland, Oregon. Her other sister flew in from Jacksonville, Florida. Her brother and sister-in-law drove up from North Carolina. They, along with another sister and some of our nieces and nephews and their children who live nearby spent time at our house laughing, sharing stories and memories, cooking and eating, and just having a tremendously joyous week. It truly was such a blessing to share time with family, who become more precious as we all age together.

Last night we were blessed to host members of our church family as our life group praised, prayed, and studied. What a powerful lesson we had on overcoming anger. We also finalized plans for our group's breakfast and lunch feeding of the homeless on December 17th.

This morning we met with our oncologist to discuss Mildred's progress. After receiving chemo on a four-week schedule, the expectation was that there would be a slight rise in her CEA. Nope. That simply is not our Father's plan. He continues to show His love for her by producing results that cannot be explained medically. Dr. Lee just shakes his head, smiles, and moves forward.

As we are now in the season of Thanksgiving and Christmas, Mildred and I are humbled by all God has done for us. At the same time, we intend to be giving to others. The more He blesses us, the more we give. Whether it is feeding and clothing the homeless, inspiring other cancer patients and their families, giving Christmas gifts and food to children and families who might not otherwise have any, we will continue to give. We simply say *thanks* and *give*.

Day 1,625 PC

Unimaginable

December 28, 2016

During the wonderful holiday season, we were so blessed. Other than Mildred's week of chemo during the first week of December, she has been full of energy and enthusiasm. We have hosted dinners at the house for friends and still have two more scheduled in early January for our salon employees and Mildred's family members who are local. She has made over 30 batches of her famous white chocolate with peanuts candy. We were able to be part of cooking and serving breakfast on two consecutive days for 68 homeless individuals. We delivered two large boxes of perishable and non-perishable food items, including 20-pound turkeys, to each of four families in need. Mike, the cancer patient we mentioned earlier, received good news that the cancer lesions on his kidneys have decreased in size. All in all, we have had a joyful and wondrous holiday season.

This morning we met with our oncologist to review Mildred's latest labs. Her weight continues to fluctuate and is currently at 108 pounds. Her latest CEA jumped to 268, over a 100-point increase. While that is disappointing, it is not alarming. Dr. Lee feels that the increase is most likely attributable to Mildred's four-week intervals between treatments over the past two months. Given her overall progress, he feels that returning to a three-week interval will lower her CEA. While we would have liked her CEA to decline, the last two wonderful months made up for it.

I had only been gone from the treatment room about 10 minutes when I received some unimaginable and horrific news. Sandra, one of the women we went to Jordan with earlier this year, suffered a loss this past Monday that I simply have no words to describe or explain. Her five-year-old grandson was playing in his family's front yard when a dump truck that had been parked and left unattended farther up the street suddenly began rolling down the street out of control. The truck rolled over her grandson and then crashed into the house. No one else was injured, but her grandson was killed upon impact. My heart aches for her, and I know that does not come close to what she must be feeling. I simply ask that each of you pray for Sandra and her family today. Pray that our Father will wrap His loving arms around them, embrace them, comfort them, and bring them peace. At a time like this, that is all any of us can stand on.

Day 1,652 PC
Difficult Days

January 24, 2017

The last couple weeks have been difficult. Mildred received her chemo treatment on December 28th and again last Wednesday, January 18th. Her CEA has increased to 319. However, the more difficult situation is the level of pain she has experienced. A little over two weeks ago, she started having constant pain in her left rib cage from front to back. After the first week, we saw our family doctor who examined her and took X-rays. The radiologist said he saw no evidence of fractures. However, when comparing this X-ray to the last X-ray of her chest in June 2016, he saw a significant increase in the cancer mass. The next day, we saw her oncologist who reviewed the radiologist's report and concurred with his findings. Mildred received her chemo that same day.

During the next few days, she did not experience any of the normal side effects of chemo. However, the pain in her rib cage escalated to the severe level. She cannot move or walk without the pain becoming debilitating. The oncologist has scheduled her next chemo treatment for next Wednesday, February 1st, two weeks after her most recent treatment. He expects to have her on a two-week treatment schedule for the next two or three treatments. During that time, her CEA will continue to be monitored. If it continues to increase, we will have to discuss alternative treatment plans because it will mean the current chemo is no longer working. In the meantime, she will have to take pain meds and see what her pain is like. The hope is that the pain and the size of the cancer will begin to decrease as the frequency of the treatments increases.

This is another one of those difficult and challenging times on our journey. I pray that our Father will bring healing to her and reduce the pain. I pray that He will decrease the cancer. I also pray that He will give me the strength to handle it all. The hardest parts of my journey have not been the physical demands but rather the times when Mildred is in pain and agony, and there is nothing I can do for her but *pray*. This is one of those times. I ask each of you to lift us up in prayer so that once again we can overcome another obstacle while continuing to walk alongside our Father.

Day 1,657 PC

New Pain Meds

January 29, 2017

Due to Mildred's severe pain, I took her to the ER on Thursday, and they did blood work and a CT. The results of the CT did not show any fractures, tears, or displacements. After the ER doctor spoke with her oncologist, their thinking is that the pain she is experiencing is the normal muscular and skeletal pain associated with her cancer and chemo. A possible reason for the increase in her pain could be that her body has developed a tolerance to the pain-related drugs she has been taking for four years, and they are no longer effective. So they decided to change her pain meds. She began taking the new meds on Friday morning. Over the past two days, her pain level has decreased somewhat, and she has slept for extended periods of time throughout the day, which is frustrating her. She is scheduled to have new labs done and receive her next chemo on Wednesday of this week. We will see then how she is doing relative to her pain and strength to determine whether she will receive her chemo.

We continue to pray for God's strength, guidance, and healing as we wrestle with living life on a two-week treatment schedule with strong pain medications and chemo side effects versus making the most of whatever time we have left. The future is in His hands.

Day 1,659 PC

I Don't Know What to Say

January 31, 2017

Since Sunday, Mildred's condition has declined. She began having diarrhea, and her physical energy and alertness decreased to the point where I took her to the oncologist this afternoon. They did a brief examination and gave her a bag of fluids to hopefully stabilize her. She definitely will not be receiving her chemo this week. Her body is too weak to handle the effects. I have to take her tomorrow morning for a set of labs and another bag of fluids. I had a brief conversation with her nurse this afternoon and am supposed to speak with her oncologist tomorrow. The short version is that if her physical condition does not improve to a level that will enable her to receive chemo, the cancer will continue to grow as it currently is. We briefly discussed the hospice process but expect to talk more about it tomorrow.

For what I believe is the first time on our journey, Mildred expressed that she is tired and does not know if she can continue. We have certainly had our share of obstacles and rough spots on our journey, but we also have had many tremendous blessings.

Somehow this feels different. I don't know what is in store for us in the days ahead, but we will continue to take each day as it arrives, putting one foot in front of the other as we march. If our Father gives Mildred's body sufficient strength and healing to continue our journey, we will do so. If He decides to call her home, we will have a joyous celebration of her life and her homegoing. As always, we rest in His loving embrace.

Day 1,660 PC

Improvement

February 1, 2017

Last night we had 18 fervent, loud prayer warriors at the house praying for Mildred and me, as well as others who are facing health issues. There were also many others not in attendance who did likewise. One of the many observations I have learned on this journey is that when an army of prayer warriors raises Mildred up to our Father, good things happen. The last time we had such a vocal army at the house was the night before her gallbladder surgery when she was given a 50/50 chance of surviving—and we all know how that turned out. While she is still tired and weak today, she has improved. She received more fluids today and is scheduled to receive more tomorrow.

She slept well last night, so all in all, her energy level and alertness are better. She was even able to minister to a woman, a client at her salon, who was receiving her first chemo treatment after undergoing surgery. You never know when someone will be placed in your path to receive blessings from you. While Mildred has improved, I am not minimizing the fact that her cancer will continue to grow, at least until she can begin receiving chemo again. We have scheduled her to have her labs on Monday, see the oncologist Wednesday morning, and then receive chemo. Of course, all this is predicated on her improvement. In the meantime, we ask each of you to please continue to pray for her. We are able to feel the strength flow through our bodies the more we are blessed to receive prayer. We truly thank every one of you.

CHARLES AND BARBARA

We met Charles and Barbara about five months ago. Charles had a lot of faith. So did Barbara, but she was afraid. Charles was very calm, but he was worried about Barbara and how fearful she was. Charles went to the doctor because he was in so much pain from pancreatic cancer. He got so bad due to the fluid building up so fast. He had to go to the hospital every two to three days to have the fluid drained. According to Barbara, he eventually got to the point where he would not eat.

About two weeks ago, Charles died. I talked with Barbara because I wanted to keep in touch with her. She said that one of Charles's brothers was with her and another was coming in from New York to stay with her for a while. I figured I would let her spend time with her brothers-in-law and then get back in touch with her. It was an honor to meet Charles and Barbara. I felt they were a blessing to Bob and me from the first evening we met them. I just want Barbara to be okay.

Day 1,667 PC
Onward!

February 8, 2017

It is no secret that the last few weeks have been difficult for Mildred and me—her for the physical pain, fatigue, and suffering, and me for seeing her go through all this and not be able to do anything except pray. This morning we met with the oncologist, and his first words were that her CEA has increased to 425—the highest since she was first diagnosed. Since April of last year, her CEA has gone from 148 to 425. That's certainly not a positive development.

Then we had the come-to-Jesus meeting. Yes, her cancer is growing. She continues to experience pain from the cancer in her lungs, particularly her left lung where the CT scan shows that the cancer nodules are growing and putting outward expanding pressure on her lung against her rib cage. Her oncologist believes that if she is willing to endure the physical pain, a combination of every two-week chemo and the use of selective radiation can decrease the growing cancer nodules. Make no mistake, it will be painful and exhausting for her, but she does not believe it is time for her to be called home. She believes she still has work to do. As long as she is willing to fight with every ounce of strength she has, then I will fight alongside her to my last breath.

Our Father put us on this journey with a purpose. Mildred's ability to minister and inspire others is magnified when the obstacles we must overcome are greatest. We *know* He will continue to be with us. As long as He continues to give us the strength to not only endure but to advance, we will continue to march. We know we have an army with us that includes each of you and all the other prayer warriors who continue to be a part of this journey. *Forward we go!*

THE PAIN INCREASES

Lately I have been in a lot of pain. The doctors thought at first that it might be a broken rib, so they sent me for X-rays, which were negative. I was in so much pain that I could hardly move. My oncologist increased my fentanyl patch to 100 mcg and also started me on Cymbalta. I already had Dilaudid at home, but I try not to use it if possible. I did not get my chemo on schedule because I was so weak. When I did get my lab work done, everything was in the normal ranges. My husband and I met with the oncologist who told us the pain is from the cancer. My CEA is at the highest it has been on this entire journey. The cancer is growing and putting pressure on my ribs.

I do not believe my Heavenly Father is ready to call me home, so I will continue to march forward. The oncologist and I agreed that we would continue the chemo treatments every two weeks. I will also get radiation on the area where the pain is located. I do not know yet when the radiation will take place, but I have an appointment for a bone scan in a few days. After the radiation and the scan, we will meet with the oncologist again. I will continue to stay on my journey until my Heavenly Father calls me home, and I do not believe it is that time yet.

Day 1,673 PC
We Continue Onward

February 14, 2017

Mildred received her chemo last Wednesday and began suffering the usual side effects over the weekend. On Monday, we met with the radiation oncologist, discussed a preliminary treatment plan, and had a bone scan. Today, after Mildred received additional fluids to stabilize her, we met again with the radiation oncologist. Her staff marked her body (target points) where the laser beams will be directed. We also were told that the bone scan did not show any signs of cancer cells. Based on this, Mildred will begin radiation treatments tomorrow and continue to receive one treatment per day for 10 consecutive days, excluding Saturday and Sunday. The objective of these treatments is to reduce or eradicate the tumors in her left lung that are pressing on her rib cage and producing constant pain. After the initial 10 days, they will reevaluate the cancer in her lung to determine whether additional radiation is necessary.

She is also scheduled to have a contrast CT scan on Friday, receive her normal labs on Monday, and then meet with her oncologist next Wednesday. He wants to have a clear picture of where the cancer currently is in her body, whether any additional radiation is warranted, and what changes, if any, might be worth implementing in her normal chemo regimen. She is scheduled to receive her next chemo treatment on Wednesday after this meeting.

These next few weeks will require a great deal of strength on Mildred's part to withstand the physical effects of everything she will undergo. While we continue to receive countless prayers from so many people, we were moved to tears earlier today when we were told that Patrick, one of our nephews who is currently a student at Virginia Tech, has arranged for an entire Catholic mass to be conducted in her name at 5:30 this afternoon at the Virginia Tech Catholic Campus Ministry. It always seems that whenever the obstacles on our journey become more difficult, we receive even more strength from everyone's prayers and thoughts. Our Father not only never forsakes us but chooses the most difficult times to let us know how much He loves us. We continue to be so blessed.

Day 1,677 PC

The Bigger the Obstacle, the Harder We Pray

February 18, 2017

After spending the afternoon in the ER, Mildred was admitted to Princess Anne Hospital tonight. The pain in her left side has increased the last few days, but the bigger issue is that she is experiencing constant vomiting and diarrhea despite taking medicine to prevent it. She has not been able to keep any nourishment down and has become dehydrated as well. After running blood work and taking a contrast CT scan, the doctors believe she has infectious, ischemic colitis. In layman's terms, she has an infection in her colon that is causing the blood flow to the colon to be restricted. They have put her on antibiotics and fluids for the next 24 to 48 hours while they monitor the situation. If there is no improvement or the situation worsens during that time, the next step will be surgery, which may result in a portion of her colon being removed. Given her history, that could result in her having a colostomy bag or worse.

She is extremely weak, tired, and hurting. She is being attacked from all sides. I pray that our Father will give her strength and heal her pain. I ask each of you and anyone else you know who prays to do so, particularly in these next couple days. A momentous chorus of prayer warriors is desperately needed right here and right now. Let us raise our voices to a feverish pitch. Our Father loves his daughter Mildred. Let us show Him how much she has inspired and loved others in His name.

Day 1,678 PC
Prayers Are Working

February 19, 2017

Unleashing an army of prayer warriors *never* fails. When I left the hospital last night and reached out to you and your prayer networks, Mildred's pain was off the charts at more than 10. In addition, she was still vomiting and experiencing diarrhea. She slept off and on overnight and awoke around noon today. Her pain this afternoon has decreased to 3 on a scale of 1 to 10. She is more alert and less fatigued. In addition, she did not have any vomiting episodes and only one diarrhea event. I had the chance to speak with most of her doctors (attending physician, oncologist, gastrointestinal doctor, surgeon), and the plan is to continue to feed her antibiotics and fluids while monitoring the infection through urine, stool samples, and blood work. Depending on how she progresses, they may run some additional tests, but they want to see what happens over the next two days.

It is no coincidence that she began to improve after everyone

I reached out to last night started praying. I am sure the voices were raised to a crescendo this morning as everyone had a chance to read my words upon waking. I know I felt the presence of the Holy Spirit this morning in church. So many of you shared with me your love and prayers for her. It also was no coincidence that one of the worship songs we sang this morning was "How Great Thou Art," one of Mildred's favorite worship songs and truly a statement of fact about our God. He is our loving Father, and I know that as we continue to lift up Mildred in prayer to HIM, SHE WILL BE HEALED.

I thank each of you for continuing to pray for us; past, present, and future. I cannot begin to adequately describe how much strength we receive through each of you. We are so blessed to have you as part of our lives. I pray that each of you will be blessed as you have blessed us.

Day 1,679 PC
Prayers Are Continuing to Work

February 20, 2017

Mildred continues to improve as prayers continue to be offered. Her pain was stable today. The pain probably will not decrease any further until the tumors pressing on her lungs and ribs are shrunk or eradicated. The doctors are still pumping antibiotics and fluids into her, and she is more alert than she was on Saturday. She is still weak and sleeps off and on, but this is an improvement from Saturday. The doctors upgraded her diet from a liquid diet to a soft foods. They hope to be able to upgrade her to a regular diet in the next 24 hours, but they are waiting to see how she does with the soft food diet. They are hoping that progress continues over the next day or so and that she might be able to come home soon.

She was able to receive visitors today. We were blessed to have one of our life group sisters come tonight and pray for us and with us. I ask everyone to please continue praying. Mildred is improving, but the battle still rages. Our army of prayer warriors stands on the front lines and will not cease or surrender. No matter what comes against us, we will overcome it with the blessings of our Father and the prayers of each of you.

Day 1,680 PC

Continued Improvement

February 21, 2017

The army of prayer warriors has once again conquered another battle. While Mildred is not completely healed yet, she had her best day in over a week today. Her pain has stabilized. She is definitely more alert and awake. She is still on a soft food diet but eating well. Her doctor hopes to advance her tomorrow to a regular food diet and oral pill form of the antibiotic she is on.

Once again, Mildred and I thank each one of you. We would not have come this far on our journey were it not for your prayers, your love, and the love of our Father. We just continue to be so blessed. Our faith strengthens more and more each time we navigate another bump in the road. Faith of steel can only come by being repeatedly tempered by fire.

Day 1,684 PC
Home Again

February 25, 2017

Mildred had a good day on Friday. The meds seemed to work as far as balancing out one versus the other. Saturday arrived, and she was relatively normal. As a result, she was able to come home on Saturday afternoon. If you eliminated the past two weeks, you would never know to look at her that she had had any problems. Her energy and alertness appear as normal as can be. Hopefully, she will feel even stronger in the morning so we can attend church and give thanks to our Father and each of you. Your prayers and His love provided the strength and healing she needed. We thank you so much.

Day 1,709 PC
March On!

March 22, 2017

These past few months certainly have been a microcosm of our journey as a whole. We continue to encounter bumps in the road, but we still march forward with the loving presence of our Father alongside us. Since Mildred was released from the hospital, she has finished her radiation and received two regular chemo treatments. The treatments continue to kick her butt as they have all along, and the fact that she is back on an every-two-week chemo schedule limits the number of days when she is feeling normal.

However, when those days have occurred, she has been able to spend some time in the salon and ministering to other patients. We spent some time with a couple we have been ministering to for a while. They are battling renal cancer and the financial fallout from being uninsured. Their house was in foreclosure but has been delayed by an attorney they have hired. The good news is that his cancer has been shrinking, and we continue to lift them up in prayer.

We march on despite the various things that come at us. The last four days, Mildred has been suffering a litany of side effects (diarrhea, fatigue, vomiting), and at the same time, I have been dealing with a sinus and chest infection that seems to be making the rounds. We both are beginning to feel better today. Mildred also needs to gain weight since she is currently down to 96 pounds, the lowest she has been. The good news, however, is that her CEA has declined from a high of 425 prior to hospitalization to 359 and just this morning to 279. We pray every day and give thanks to our Father and to each of you. Only through your prayers and His love are we able to continue to march on, and *march on we will!*

Day 1,730 PC

Status Quo

April 12, 2017

The past month has been difficult for us, but we are marching forward. Mildred is on the two-week interval for treatments, which means it takes longer for her to recover. After each treatment, the side effects, particularly the diarrhea, begin. Despite taking two different anti-diarrhea medicines, they are unable to stop the diarrhea. She experiences these side effects for most of the two weeks between treatments. The day or two before her next treatment, she seems to be as normal as possible, but she has suffered and lost weight.

We met with the oncologist earlier today to review her status. He prescribed a different anti-diarrhea medicine that she has not taken before. Her weight today is down to 94 pounds as a result of not being able to retain food and nutrients. During the past month, her CEA has increased from 279 to 351, and then today it was down to 301. As a result, she will stay on the two-week interval in an attempt to establish a downward trend of the cancer.

Aside from her cancer issues, during the past month we have had various things—both at home and the salon—crash and burn. Needless to say, we have had our hands full dealing with these issues. I would not be honest if I said the sum of everything has not had any effect on us. But during the roughest of times, we have managed to persevere, drawing upon the strength our Father has given us each day. We know that the more we suffer attacks, the stronger our faith becomes. If in any way we are able to inspire others through these attacks, then the reality is that each attack becomes a blessing, and for that we are extremely grateful.

Day 1,734 PC

How Much More?

April 16, 2017

Saturday evening, aside from her usual chemo side effects, Mildred began to complain of physical pain in her stomach and throat, accompanied by a burning and acid-like sensation. We attempted to treat the symptoms with an over-the-counter antacid but to no avail. Finally around 5:00 a.m., Mildred agreed to go to the Princess Anne Hospital ER. We were admitted at 6:00 a.m., and they began a series of blood work, tests, and scans to determine what was happening. The preliminary diagnosis was that she has a severe infection in her throat, esophagus, and stomach that is causing the pain and burning sensations. Her white blood count was seven times higher than the high end of the normal range.

Both her attending physician and her regular GI doctor reviewed the tests and spoke with me. Their primary concern, along with mine, is that she may have thrush, the fungal infection she had in October 2012, two months after she began chemo. It has the potential to not only irritate but eat away the interior lining of her esophagus. It was potentially life-threatening back then, and it is now.

They have scheduled a series of procedures on Monday, including an endoscopy where they run a camera down her throat and into her stomach to get a visual of what is wrong. In the meantime, they are pumping her with antibiotics and pain meds to try to combat any infection until they have more precise information. She has been sleeping or awake but disoriented throughout the day. She has been admitted to the hospital, but there are currently no beds available, and they are putting their admissions in the ER. The hope is that a bed upstairs will become available sometime overnight.

We will see what tomorrow brings. I do not know how much more Mildred's body can handle. Her immune system has been so compromised that infections are occurring more frequently. Her weight remains low at 94. Her energy level is significantly less than it was one year ago, but if she does not continue chemo, she will succumb sooner than later. I know our Father can heal her, but how He chooses to do so is His will, not ours. I pray that He will heal her either way and will not let her continue to suffer. I will rejoice in whatever manner of healing He chooses. If He removes the infections from her body so she can continue her mission, great! If He calls her home, that is also great for she will be free of pain. I will love her always and forever, as we pledged to each other 37 years ago. I know that whatever happens, we will reside together in His loving embrace.

Day 1,735 PC

Pain and Suffering

April 17, 2017

Mildred was moved to a regular room last night. She continues to experience significant pain in her abdominal cavity, throat, and esophagus when she is awake. She is still getting antibiotics, pain meds, and fluids. The result is that she sleeps most of the day. When she is awake, she is disoriented and usually falls back to sleep in a few minutes. Between the normal chemo side effects and the infection, her body is exhausted as it continues to fight.

There are a couple things from today, one good and one not so good. Her white count went down from 74K to 52K, still well above the 10.9K upper level for normal but at least a step in the right direction. She had the endoscopy this afternoon. It revealed a significant level of infection and irritation in her throat, esophagus, and stomach. It also revealed a moderate level of thrush. They took some tissue samples and sent them off for biopsy. As a result of the thrush, they added another antibiotic to her IV regimen and prescribed a swish-and-swallow medicine to coat the inner linings and hopefully prevent the spread of the thrush.

I sat with her most of the day. I think the most difficult events of our entire almost five-year journey have been watching her on days like this. To see her suffer and her body so racked with discomfort and pain breaks my heart. I so want to ease her pain, to take it for her, and yet there is nothing I can do other than pray. I continue to pray that God will not let her suffer. I pray that He will heal her and set her back on her journey and mission, or take her home, but please do not let her suffer.

Day 1,736 PC

Positive Steps

April 18, 2017

Today was a small step forward with no steps back. Mildred slept off and on and was awake for longer periods of time. She was more alert and aware. When we came to the ER on Sunday, she rated her pain as a 10. On Monday, she rated it an 8, and today it was a 5—still present but not as severe. Her white count declined to 35K, well above the normal of 10.9K but headed in the right direction. She is still on a totally liquid diet but was able to keep down what she ate. Yesterday she was vomiting frequently, but today only once. All in all, it was a better day than yesterday.

We will see what tomorrow brings, but I continue to pray that God will heal her in whatever way He chooses. We both thank all of you for your continued prayers and love. Again, whenever we encounter these types of situations, it is our army of prayer warriors who provide us the strength from our Father that enables us to continue. We are blessed.

Day 1,738 PC

Best Day Yet

April 20, 2017

Mildred continued to improve today. Her white count is back in normal ranges. Her pain is a 4. She remains on a soft food diet with no vomiting. She was able to sit up, converse, and take one or two naps but not continuous sleeping. The prognosis is still for her to come home on Saturday, followed by three to five days of home care. Today was also the first day she was up for having visitors, which she did.

Once again, our loving Father has healed her pain and suffering and placed her back on her mission of inspiring and helping others. In fact, one of her visitors shared news of a couple in their 40s who was recently told the husband has Stage 4 colon cancer and is seeing the same oncology practice as we are. We gave him a couple of our Voices of Hope flyers and let them know we are available to help in any way.

We have been through many major bumps in the road, but I am still amazed at what God does for Mildred. Having witnessed the pain and suffering she experienced this past Sunday and Monday and then to see her today, she is truly a living example of our Father's love. We are experiencing the miracle of healing on this journey, something that is far above anything I could ever have imagined. What a joy! What a blessing!

Day 1,739 PC
A Plateau

April 21, 2017

Today was a plateau day—nothing improved. Her pain level remained at a 4. She slept more than she did on Thursday. She is still on a soft food diet. Her platelet count has been at 46—49 for the last three days. The doctors will not send her home without additional improvement as they are afraid she may fall and then bleed out due to the low platelet count. In addition, they want to see her be able to walk unassisted. As a result, they will be keeping her in the hospital at least until Sunday and more likely Monday. We will keep praying for additional healing and strength.

Day 1,742 PC
Maybe

April 24, 2017

Mildred had the best day of her now nine-day stay in the hospital. When I arrived at her room, she was sitting in the recliner watching TV. She had taken a walk with her physical therapist completely around the fourth floor. Her platelets have increased to 111. While not ready to run a marathon, she appeared to have more energy and spark than any other day. She was alert and able to converse. Her attending physician told her that if her Tuesday morning labs and doctor visit reflect continued improvement, she will be able to go home. She will still have a few days of rest after she arrives home, but the immediate future appears positive.

Thank you to all of you for your continued prayers and love.

Day 1,743 PC

Home!

April 25, 2017

I just finished getting Mildred home and settled. She is still very tired. The doctors want her to limit her physical movement for at least the next five days as she recuperates. We are scheduled to meet with her oncologist on Wednesday and discuss a treatment plan and schedule, particularly in view of this recent episode.

Again, thank you for your prayers and love.

Day 1,751 PC

Treading Water

May 3, 2017

Mildred has been home from the hospital for a week now. She has spent the time mostly resting and regaining her strength. This morning we met with her oncologist to review where she is at and her ongoing treatment. Her weight is the same at 94 pounds. It is a good sign that she hasn't lost more weight. Her blood work, with the exception of her white count that is slightly elevated, is all in the normal ranges. She will have new labs on Friday to determine if her white count remains elevated. Her CEA is up slightly, increasing from 301 to 319. However, the cumulative findings of the three consecutive CT scans she has had since January 1st show no significant change—positive or negative—in her cancer.

Due to her hospitalization, she had a three-week interval between her last chemo treatment and the one she is receiving today. Mildred and I, as well as Dr. Lee, are in a quandary as to whether she should continue to receive treatment on a three-week basis—giving her body more time to recover—or have two-week treatments, thereby fighting the cancer more aggressively. The consensus we came to was to simply take it one treatment at a time. We all feel that the higher priority right now is to give her body as much rest as possible. When we get to the next treatment, we will reevaluate everything and make a decision.

Dr. Lee referred to Mildred today as a Super Ball—a ball made of material that enables it to keep bouncing. He said she continues to bounce back from whatever situations she encounters, no matter how difficult. While that is true, it is her supreme level of faith that enables her to do so. No matter how much pain and physical difficulties she encounters, she draws closer to her Heavenly Father as the situation becomes more difficult. She has not wavered on this journey. Not once has she ever said it is time to end this. She continues to know that God will let her know whenever that time comes, but until then, she will continue to march forward, overcoming whatever obstacles are placed in front of her. She has been not only a blessing but truly a source of inspiration and faith. If she can continue to march forward with all that she has, how can any of us wilt in our own faith? She is truly a special angel to each of us.

Day 1,772 PC
O Ye of Little Faith

May 24, 2017

As you know, these past few months have been physically difficult for Mildred with her two hospitalizations and various symptoms and side effects. Since her hospital discharge, she has fallen twice and nearly fallen another time due to dizziness and loss of balance. She has consistently experienced an immediate drop in blood pressure of 20 or more points when going from a sitting to standing position. She has experienced episodes of disorientation with regard to what day or time it is and where she is. Some days she has been asleep more hours than she has been awake. She is losing weight, now currently at 90 pounds.

It is so hard to see her undergo all these things. Her physical appearance resembles a malnourished Syrian refugee. We were not able to return to Jordan this year. Part of our team arrived home just yesterday. All this has made me fear that we are now on the last leg of our cancer journey. However, not Mildred. She has never wavered.

Today we met with her oncologist, and once again her faith has been rewarded. She had an MRI a little over a week ago to determine if there was any cancer or other issues in her head. The MRI was totally clean—no cancer—like a normal 68-year-old woman. Her CEA is 251, the lowest since late last year.

Her doctor plans to keep her on a three-week interval for chemo treatments as long as the CEA does not significantly increase. He believes her blood pressure issues may be related to the steroids she has been taking since the beginning of her chemo. He thinks her adrenal gland's ability to produce a hormone (cortisol) that helps regulate the flow of blood may have been negatively affected by the steroids. As a result, he is going to start her on a pill supplement form of cortisol and monitor the results over the next three to six weeks. If the symptoms continue, he will have her evaluated by a cardiologist. All in all, he did not consider it anything to worry about.

Faith is believing in what you cannot see. But often we allow what we *can* see to overwhelm us and cause fear and anxiety. I have to plead guilty to that. As many times as God has picked us up and carried us, my fear and love for Mildred has gotten the best of me. She has said from the beginning that God will let her know when it is time for her to go home. He has not yet done that. In fact, He continues to provide her with ministry opportunities. While she was in the waiting room, she was able to minister to a patient who has been battling breast cancer for 17 years (since she was 23) and feels she just cannot do this anymore. She also spent time ministering to a 43-year-old patient who also has Stage 4 colon cancer. When she went back to the treatment room to receive chemo, there was an empty chair between these two patients. Needless to say, she seated herself there and continued ministering. In addition, Mike, who we have been ministering to for a while now in his battle with renal cancer, came into the treatment room, saw her, and spent some time with her. When you watch how these situations occur, we just have to know that *He still has this*!

There simply is no other way to explain it.

Day 1,793 PC
Continued Thanks and Faith

June 14, 2017

We met with Dr. Lee, our oncologist, earlier this morning. We have so much to be thankful for. Mildred's weight has increased to 99 pounds and should continue to increase with the medication she is taking. All her regular lab work is in normal ranges. The best number is her CEA of 199, more than a 50 percent decrease. She has only had one episode of dizziness and loss of balance in the past three weeks since we saw Dr. Lee. He has scheduled an appointment for next Wednesday with a cardiologist to try to determine what the cause may be. Once again Dr. Lee just marvels at her, calling her "unique." He gets a big grin on his face when he sees her. I know he is as inspired by her as are the patients she ministers to.

We have certainly had our share of challenges so far this year, and there certainly have been times when fear has gripped me. But it is days like today when my strength and faith are renewed. While Mildred simply has an unshakable, unmovable level of faith, my faith is still growing. She has a relationship with our Father that very few of us ever achieve. In Old Testament days, we would call her one of the prophets for she is able to receive and communicate with God in a way that most of us cannot. I have to keep telling myself that as long as He has not told her that her work here is done and He is ready to call her home, He will take us through this no matter what comes our way.

Day 1,814 PC
Continuing Forward

July 5, 2017

We met with Mildred's oncologist today before she received her next round of chemo. Once again, the news was positive. Her labs were all in the normal ranges, and her CEA has decreased to 188. Her weight still needs to increase but is holding steady at 98 pounds. She was able to visit the salon for a few hours on Saturday and go to church on Sunday, followed by brunch with some friends. She also was able to do some things around the house. That helps her feel normal.

In 12 days (July 17th) we will celebrate her five-year anniversary since being diagnosed. It is incredible that we have been on this journey for five years and are still going strong and moving forward. We have met and lost so many people along the way, and yet here we are. The surgeon's words five years ago still resonate with me—"Get her affairs in order; she will be lucky to live two years." Our Father clearly did not share the surgeon's assessment. As we continue onward, we pray that He will continue to bless us and enable us to bless all we come in contact with. May His love radiate forth from us and provide strength and healing to everyone.

Day 1,833 PC

Another Test of Faith

July 24, 2017

For the most part, Mildred has done all right these last three weeks since her chemo. She developed some pneumonia the first few days after the treatment but was placed on an antibiotic right away, which helped her overcome it. Her weight has remained stable in the 90-pound-plus range, and her labs are in the normal ranges. However, she began experiencing pain again in her left side in the area of her lungs, heart, and ribs. She had a new CT scan this past Friday.

The results of the CT were definitely not what we expected. While the bulk of the cancer in her body has been stable or in some cases decreased in size, the cancer in her left side has increased 78 percent compared to the January 2017 CT scan. More importantly, the cancer has entered her third rib bone and has attached itself to her fourth rib bone. In addition, her pleural cavity in that area has thickened, which may be a contributing factor to her heart and blood pressure issues.

Needless to say, none of her doctors expected this. We spoke with her oncologist and the physician assistant by phone today. Mildred will receive her normal chemo this Wednesday as scheduled. However, we have a meeting tomorrow afternoon with the radiation oncologist to discuss the scan and a plan of radiation to attack this latest explosion. Her oncologist said that once the cancer penetrates the bones, radiation is the only curative form of treatment available. If that does not work, they can manage her pain but will not be able to stop the cancer. We also have a meeting tomorrow with her cardiologist to review the findings of his tests and monitoring over the last month.

I don't know exactly what words can describe what I feel this afternoon. I know we have a greater sense of urgency about some things than we did before today. However, I also know that *God still has this*! He has had it from the beginning and has remained faithful to us throughout this entire journey. Can I say for sure what the outcome will be? Of course not. I can say, though, that fear is not one of the emotions we are feeling right now. No matter what, we wrap ourselves in His loving embrace and continue to stand on the rock of faith in Him. Our faith has seen us through every step of this journey. Time and time again, the obstacles we have faced have resulted in God being *glorified*. We do not expect anything different this time. We continue to covet your prayers, and we rest in His will.

Day 1,846 PC

Please Pray

August 6, 2017

It has been two weeks since we found out that the cancer has moved into Mildred's third rib bone and attached to the fourth rib. Since that time, she has had her normal chemo regimen and subsequent fluids. In addition, she began two weeks of radiation treatments this past Thursday. We are scheduled to meet again with the radiation oncologist on Wednesday and our regular oncologist, Dr. Lee, on Thursday. Her weight is declining, currently at 89 pounds.

The most difficult part is the amount of pain she is in. Yesterday afternoon on the way to receive her fluid infusion, she suddenly had a sharp, driving pain from her left shoulder to the fingertips on her left hand. That is the side the cancer and radiation are on. Mildred can handle a significant amount of pain, but this pain brought her to tears and rendered her unable to move her left arm without a severe increase in the pain. The pain is constant but increases with any movement. In addition to the daily pain patch she wears, she receives a second pain med every four hours. Earlier this evening, I put her left arm in a medical sling we had to take some of the weight off her arm, but she is still hurting. While receiving her infusion today, we spoke with the nurse, who in turn spoke with Dr. Lee. The short answer is that other than pain medication, there is nothing they can do at the moment. When we meet on Wednesday and Thursday, the doctors will examine her arm and ribs, test the pain, and see if anything can be done other than medicating her so significantly that she will have limited awareness of what is happening around her.

Please pray for us tonight. I cannot stand to see her suffer in pain and not be able to do anything to help her. I have prayed before and I pray again that God will give me the pain and remove it from her. I beg Him to not let her suffer. The tears flow from my eyes as I write this because she is hurting so much. Please pray for her healing, our strength, and most of all, His *peace*.

Day 1,847 PC

Keep Praying

August 7, 2017

Mildred is still in pain but we were able to move up her next radiation treatment to today. Dr. Bonner, the radiation oncologist, believes the pain is being caused by the cancer in the rib bones and is being augmented by the radiation treatments. She will discuss her findings with Dr. Lee before he meets with us on Thursday. At that time, we will discuss possible changes to her chemo regimen. In the meantime, Dr. Bonner has doubled the dosage of Mildred's pain pill that she receives every four hours, increased the level of her pain patch, and increased the frequency and dosage of her neuropathy medicine. Dr. Bonner believes the combination of these changes will help decrease the level of pain Mildred is experiencing but will most likely make her less aware of what is going on around her. Right now, that is a trade-off we will gladly accept. We continue to covet your prayers as we march forward one day, one step at a time, resting in our loving Father's embrace.

Day 1,851 PC

Keep Marching

August 11, 2017

The increased pain medications have made a significant difference in Mildred's pain. Within 24 hours, her pain began to moderate.

Yesterday when we met with her oncologist, the pain was a 5 or 6 instead of a 10+. Typical Mildred, she can handle that level of pain, so she stopped taking the four-hour pain med. As of today, she only has the stronger pain patch. She has received radiation every day this week and will finish her radiation cycle next Wednesday. She also will receive her next chemo treatment that day, along with updated CEA and lab numbers.

We spent an hour with Dr. Lee yesterday looking at her latest CT scan and reviewing the current positioning of the cancer in her lungs and now rib bones. He is cautiously optimistic that the combination of her radiation and chemo will shrink the cancer in her ribs, as well as result in another downward trend in her CEA. We talked about other chemo regimens, the frequency of her chemo treatments, new cancer drugs that are entering the marketplace, and two current colon cancer clinical trials that Virginia Oncology Associates is running in conjunction with the researchers at Duke University. The bottom line from his view is that given her treatment history, her results, and her attitude and faith, we have a number of options to choose from, even if a treatment change is necessary. He wants to see what her CEA is next week and three weeks out, along with the radiation results. If a downward, decreasing trend results, we will continue her current treatment. If her CEA shows an upward, increasing trend, we will change the chemo regimen to one of the options we discussed. His belief is that it is more likely that Mildred will respond better to some form of chemo rather than any of the other options.

So *we keep marching*! While these past few weeks have produced another obstacle to overcome, *we will overcome it*! God continues to walk alongside us and provide us with the necessary strength. Despite the initial punch in the gut, He has always brought us over each obstacle. This one will be no different. We thank each of you for your continued prayers and love.

Day 1,856 PC

The Obstacle Is Getting Larger

August 16, 2017

We met with Mildred's radiation oncologist and her oncologist today. Mildred received the last of the 10 consecutive radiation treatments today. Those treatments, along with the increase in her pain meds, definitely made a difference in her pain, which is down to a 3 today. She began returning to her normal dose levels in the last few days and can handle a level 3 pain. At that point, it is really just an annoyance. When she receives her next scan, she may need additional radiation, but they will monitor her until then.

When we met with Dr. Lee, he said her CEA has risen to a 394. That is a significant jump from three weeks ago when it was 228. While the rise certainly could be a sign that the cancer is growing, he feels it is more likely a result of the radiation treatments attacking the cancer. In essence, the radiation makes the cancer more active in the radiated area(s), which in turn causes it to produce more of the protein that is the base of the CEA measurement. Mildred received her chemo with a few tweaks in the medicines today. Dr. Lee wants to see what her CEA is next time, now that she is finished with radiation. He also wants to do a new biopsy of the cancer to know whether or not there have been any changes in the genetic composition of her cancer that would alter the chemo treatments she has been receiving.

In summary, we have a larger obstacle to overcome compared to where we were six or seven weeks ago. However, it just means we have to pray harder and draw in even closer to our Father's loving embrace. The bigger the obstacle to overcome, the bigger the victory. We will continue to march forward, and nothing the enemy puts in our path will stop us.

Day 1,898 PC

Treading Water Again

September 27, 2017

If any of you have ever tread water for a long period of time, you know that you are paddling, attempting to keep your head above water, without actually going anywhere. That is what the last two months have felt like. Mildred's weight has remained in the 90—95 pound range. She has had a level of pain in her rib where the cancer has invaded the bone, some days minimal and other days off the charts. This past week, I had to double-dose her pain med for a couple days because the pain was so excruciating that she was in tears. She has continued to receive her chemo treatments every three weeks, including today. However, her CEA has continued to increase, ranging from a low of 188 in early July to 444 today. The day she was diagnosed, her CEA was 451.

While we have had an incredible journey these last five years, we have now come full circle back to where we started. Having observed the upward trend in her CEA, Dr. Lee ordered a biopsy to confirm the genetic characteristics of her existing cancer in order to determine what other forms of treatment, primarily pills or clinical drug trials, she might be compatible with. The results showed that she has a couple gene mutations that exclude some of the more widely used treatment drugs she would otherwise be eligible for. The end result is that there are very few treatment drugs or clinical trials that might be options, and their success rates range from 5-20 percent. She has had both the FOLFOX and the FOLFIRI treatment regimens, both with issues of strength versus pain.

Dr. Lee decided that Mildred should have a new PET scan to know for sure exactly where and what size her cancer is before making any change of treatment. So we will continue to tread water these next three weeks. We will continue to pray for strength and healing. We have said from the beginning that God has this, and nothing has changed our belief. No matter what the outcome, we rest in His loving embrace. "Even though I walk through the darkest valley of the shadow of death, I will fear no evil, for you are with me" (Ps. 23:4, NIV).

Day 1,919 PC

Continuing to Tread Water

October 18, 2017

We met with Dr. Lee this morning. Mildred's CEA is up slightly to 466. The PET scan shows no evidence of any new cancer cells but does show some slight increases in the size of cancer lesions that were present on her scan last year. Her weight has decreased to 84 pounds. Dr. Lee decided to wait until our next meeting in three weeks before making any change of treatment decisions. In the meantime, he wants to have another biopsy done, this time looking for two distinct genetic characteristics that, if present, will make her cancer compatible with two drugs that are currently in trials. In addition, she will have to get an updated MRI on her brain to ensure that none of the cancer in her lungs has migrated to her brain. So we continue to wait. While it feels like one step forward and one step backward, going nowhere, we know that God still has this. As it has been the entire journey—*His time, His plan.*

Day 1,940 PC

One Step Forward, Two Steps Backward

November 8, 2017

These last few weeks have been physically challenging. Mildred's weight remains at 84 pounds, which is a 96-pound weight loss since the day she was diagnosed. Her daily fatigue level continues to increase. Any significant exertion, even going to lunch with a friend, results in her being overwhelmed with fatigue throughout the remainder of the day and falling asleep by early evening. She has had difficulty keeping food down and has vomiting spells that last for two to three days.

We were scheduled to meet with Dr. Lee today to review the MRI, the biopsy, and the genetic testing results. However, he postponed the meeting until next Wednesday. They are still conducting genetic testing on the tissue they obtained from her most recent biopsy. As of now, they have not found a genetically compatible drug or trial, but they are still looking. In the meantime, her CEA has risen to 525, the highest since she was first diagnosed.

Dr. Lee believes that until they find the right drug and trial, it is better to keep giving her the existing chemo and thus slow the cancer's growth rate than skip the chemo treatments all together and let the cancer grow unchecked.

Despite these latest events, we continue to *march on*. Until our Father causes Mildred to take her last breath, we will continue to go forward. We continue to pray for His healing, recognizing that healing may come in a manner that removes her from this world and takes her home. Or He may truly work another miracle and continue to propel us forward in our ministry. We accepted long ago that He is in control of this journey, and we will accept whatever He has in store for us. Either way, we are embraced in His loving arms.

Day 1,947 PC

He Still Has This!

November 15, 2017

We met with Dr. Lee this afternoon to review the various test results and discuss where we are. The good news is that the MRI was clear, thus confirming that none of the cancer has spread to Mildred's brain. However, the genetic testing of the tissue from the two biopsies did not produce any current forms of treatment that would be genetically compatible with her cancer. That leaves chemo as the only form of treatment. She can continue to slow the rate of growth of the cancer by taking the FOLFIRI regimen, but it appears that it will not prevent the cancer from growing, just slow the rate. The other possibility is to change back to the FOLFOX regimen she was taking during the first few months of treatment in the fall of 2012.

The consensus of the three of us is to take the lower strength FOLFOX she last received and see how she handles it. When she changed from FOLFOX to FOLFIRI it was because she could not handle the side effects of FOLFOX, even at a lower strength. That may still be the case, but the only way to find out is to try it. If she can handle it, she will receive two more treatments, possibly at an increased strength. After three FOLFOX treatments, we will see whether her CEA is still increasing or possibly decreasing. One positive factor in using the FOLFOX this time is that she will be on a three-week treatment schedule. When she was taking FOLFOX in 2012, she was on a two-week schedule. Hopefully, the extra week will give her body sufficient time to recover before the next treatment.

Another decision we made today was to have her seen by the colon cancer specialists at Duke University with whom Dr. Lee has a long-standing personal relationship. The plan is to schedule a trip to Duke in the latter half of January after she has received the three FOLFOX treatments. That will enable all of us, including the specialists at Duke, to know whether the FOLFOX will work. Even if it works, the plan is to conduct more sophisticated and specialized tests on her cancer and determine whether there are any other treatment options, including possible upcoming trials.

Some might read all the above info and feel sadness or fear. But we have neither of those feelings. Instead, we continue to rest in God's embrace and do not yet believe He is ready to call her home. We believe this is just another obstacle to further demonstrate His love and power. We will continue to minister to and inspire others on their cancer journeys. *We will not quit!* As long as we have His strength and love to support us, we will continue to *march on.* We have been so blessed by your words and actions that we will be forever grateful. *Onward we go!*

Day 1,961 PC

Positive Signs

November 29, 2017

We met with Dr. Lee today before Mildred received her chemo. Two positives emerged:

1. Her weight increased to 90.6 pounds. It is the first time she has been in the 90s over the last couple months. I guess we will have to have Thanksgiving dinner every week.

2. Her CEA, prior to receiving chemo today, decreased to 471 from 525.

There is no medical explanation for why her CEA decreased. Today was the first day she began receiving the FOLFOX chemo regimen, and we will see what happens over the next three treatments and determine whether a trend, be it positive or negative, emerges. In the meantime, we continue to put our faith in our Father and His healing capabilities. He has been and will continue to be, along with each of you, our source of strength. The number of prayers on our behalf continues to intensify, and we remain so thankful.

Day 1,967 PC

Heartache

December 5, 2017

Since Mildred received her chemo last week, we have had some rough days. She was okay the first day but then began to suffer the chemo side effects with severe fatigue and loss of appetite. She has slept off and on since Saturday.

Another obstacle confronted us today. Late this morning, Hope—our beloved 13-year-old golden retriever—died. She had a large tumor that, given her age and condition, was inoperable. At about 11:00 this morning, she had a seizure that lasted a minute or two, and then she passed. Fortunately, Mildred and I were both there to comfort her as she left this world. I do not consider myself a qualified theologian to say whether there is a place in our God's heaven for our beloved pets, but I know that Mildred and I find comfort in believing that we will see each of our three much-loved pets that we have buried in our 37 years of marriage. Our hearts ache as we suffer the pain of loss, but we continue to pray for His healing love and grace.

Day 1,973 PC

Fervent Prayers

December 11, 2017

This past week has been a struggle for us. After our golden retriever died, Mildred developed a respiratory infection. I took her to our primary care physician late Friday afternoon. After examining her and taking chest X-rays, he did not see any pneumonia, but she does have an infection. He put her on an antibiotic and expectorant to combat the infection and mucous buildup in her lungs. In addition, her heart rate is elevated as a result of the infection. While her current rate is not life-threatening, if it continues to increase, she will require hospital treatment and testing. She is also experiencing severe fatigue from the chemo and sleeping more than she is awake. She has had intermittent vomiting, and the pain in her left side where the cancer invaded her rib bone has returned. Her weight yesterday had declined to 86 pounds.

Everything is coming at us all at once. As I have said over the course of this five-and-a-half-year journey, it is only through the strength God provides us and through the prayers each of you and many, many others have raised up on our behalf that we have been able to continue marching forward. Whenever we have had our roughest times on the journey, it has been the fervent prayers of the army of prayer warriors such as you that surround us and lift us up. This is one of those times. I ask not just for prayer but for *fervent prayers* to give us strength, to give Mildred healing, and to enable us to continue marching on. It has been during times such as this that the power of prayer has been most evident, and we are seeking it now. Please raise your voices in loud, fervent prayers on our behalf to our Father.

Day 1,982 PC

Watch What I Do Now

December 20, 2017

These last few weeks have been hard with the loss of our beloved dog and with Mildred's suffering through the side effects of the chemo. She has had intermittent vomiting and diarrhea, and severe fatigue. She was unable to attend either of the salon's open houses the last two Saturdays to thank our clients for their continued support. She was only able to make one small batch of her favorite white chocolate peanut candies.

From this past Saturday evening until early Monday morning, she slept approximately 30 hours during a 36-hour period. Although she did not sleep as much this Monday and Tuesday, she still felt weak and was only able to go out to have her lab work done on Monday.

Today, it was as if our loving Father breathed His air into Mildred's nostrils. Her energy level is markedly improved. We just finished meeting with Dr. Lee and reviewed her labs. As you know, when we last met with him three weeks ago, prior to Mildred receiving the chemo, her CEA had decreased from 525 to 471. It was as if God was saying, don't be confused by the medicine but instead understand that *I am still at work here. Watch what I do now!* Her labs show that her CEA has once again decreased from 471 to 435. The fervent prayers of all our prayer warriors have once again been heard by our Father, and He has responded once more.

I cannot adequately describe in words the *joy* that once again we are able to experience. While our journey has had and will continue to have obstacles and rough spots, we are marching forward, and our loving Father is marching with us. Sometimes He still picks us up and carries us, particularly me when my fears begin to work on me.

God and each of our prayer warriors continue to provide the strength we need to continue the journey. We are blessed beyond anything we deserve, and we are so thankful. Have a Merry Christmas!

Day 1,987 PC

Another Obstacle

December 25, 2017

Mildred's condition began to deteriorate over the last few days, resulting in her having to be taken by ambulance Christmas morning to Princess Anne Hospital. She was semi-conscious with severe pain on both her left and right sides, congestion in her lungs, dehydration, and intermittent vomiting. After labs, CT scans, X-rays, and more, the doctors determined a couple things. First, her white blood count, which should normally be 4,100—10,900, was in excess of 100,000, signifying the presence of severe infection. Second, and the more significant issue, they found that the cancer has expanded in both the left and right sides of her lungs and chest cavity. New cancer lesions were found in her liver. The cancer in her lungs has attacked tissue in both lungs, causing holes and allowing air to escape into her chest cavity. That is why her heart rate has been elevated these last few weeks.

The only long-term cure for this in a normal patient is cardiothoracic surgery. Given her physical condition, the belief is that she would never survive the surgery. Even if the surgery were successful, without solving the underlying cause of the problem—the cancer—the condition would quickly return.

She has been admitted to the hospital, and the doctors are attempting to stabilize her condition in the short term with IVs of powerful antibiotics to combat the infection(s). She is also on an oxygen mask that is pumping 100 percent pure oxygen into her lungs to facilitate breathing. They are waiting on the results of a barium swallowing test to determine if there are any additional holes in her esophagus. If there are no additional holes, they will give her some type of coating medicine to try to cover the inner linings of her lungs and temporarily seal the holes. The only other option available, according to her team of doctors, is to intubate her with a breathing tube. That discussion led to discussing what her wishes are in terms of any advanced care directive (ACD) or do not resuscitate (DNR) order. I made it known to them that we both have on file with the hospital system our ACDs that speak to what we want and do not want in the event of life-threatening conditions. They also brought up the subject of hospice care, which would mean the end of cancer treatment and transitioning to palliative care. Clearly, the fact that these two subjects were brought up indicates the seriousness of her current condition.

I hope to discuss her current medical condition with her oncologist tomorrow and hear what his perspective is on continuing care in light of these most recent events. After that, Mildred and I will speak with her hospital doctors to determine what is next. In the meantime, I am praying for guidance, wisdom, and strength from our Heavenly Father about what He would have us do. I also am praying that He will not let Mildred suffer. If He intends to call her home, I pray He will do so quickly. If He intends to continue healing her, then let it be done. He has had this journey from the beginning, and I know He still has it. Whatever form of healing He chooses, Mildred and I will embrace it. We sincerely ask for your prayers tonight, as well as anyone you know who would be willing to pray for her. We remain in His hands.

Day 1,988 PC

Small Steps

December 26, 2017

Mildred was able to take some small steps forward today. Her white blood count is down to 60,000 from 100,000, with the target being 10,000. The barium swallowing test showed no tears or holes in her esophagus. They were able to remove the oxygen mask this morning and substitute the standard nasal line to pump oxygen into her. The objective is that she will be able to breathe on her own. With some changes in her pain medications, they were able to reduce the level of pain in both her left and right sides. The pain is still there but is tolerable rather than severe as it was yesterday. They also have her on a liquid diet since whenever she tried to swallow anything solid, it resulted in her coughing, vomiting, and irritating the infected areas. They have also converted all her medications to an IV equivalent to be administered intravenously. Her weight as of this morning was 76.3 pounds.

Her team of doctors includes her cardiologist, a pulmonary doctor, a pain management doctor, her oncologist, and the hospital's attending physician. The consensus at this moment is to focus on getting her stabilized and back to her normal. When that occurs, the decisions concerning what to do next and whether she can or will continue chemo treatment will need to be made. She is still very tired and weak, unable to get out of bed without assistance. However, she is more aware and alert and able to comprehend what is being said.

Thank you to our army of prayer warriors who have supported us these last 24 hours. Our strength comes from the prayers being offered, and we know our Father is hearing the loud, passionate voices of a large army. We thank each of you and seek your continued engagement as we move forward.

Day 1,990 PC

More Steps

December 28, 2017

Mildred continues to show gradual improvement from one day to the next. She is definitely more awake and alert than she was Christmas morning when she was admitted. As of this morning (Thursday), her white count is down to 25,000 from the original 100,000+. Her pain in her left and right sides, while still present, has decreased to a 3 on a scale of 1 to 10. She is still on a liquid diet, but her appetite has improved, and she has gained 5 pounds in the past two days, now weighing 81 pounds. Her platelet count has improved to 88 from 37, with 130 being the target number. Her electrolytes continue to improve.

They have been taking daily morning X-rays of her chest and

lungs, and each one has been slightly better than the previous one. She still has some nausea and vomiting but less than when she was admitted. Once she is home, we will schedule a meeting with her oncologist to discuss what we do next regarding treatments, be it chemo or otherwise.

Once again, the power of prayer has prevailed. Given the condition she was in Christmas morning and her condition early this morning, our Father has clearly heard the loud cries of his faithful children and blessed her with healing to this point. We continue to seek everyone's prayers for strength and blessing. I cannot imagine how we could have navigated this journey without the love and prayers each of you has given us. Again, we are so grateful.

Day 1,991 PC

Home

December 28, 2017

Slightly to our surprise, Mildred was sent home this evening. After discussing her condition with her pulmonary doctor, cardiologist, and attending physician, their consensus was that her condition would not be any better by staying in the hospital longer versus being able to be home and comfortable in her own surroundings. The one caveat to this is that she will be on oxygen 24/7 for the short term and quite possibly for the remainder of her life.

We arrived home at about 8:00 p.m. The oxygen company personnel arrived about 8:30 p.m. and got her set up with a large, electrically powered oxygen machine and also a portable tank and cart. She will use the electrical machine when she is at home and the portable one when she leaves the house. Once they finished, I took Mildred upstairs, and she went right to sleep, which is probably the best thing for her given all the strain her body has experienced this past week.

Over the next week, the main goal is to build her back up to her normal level and then meet with her oncologist to discuss the future plan of treatment, be it continued chemo or some form of hospice. I pray that she regains her strength and is able to have some measure of quality of life without continued suffering. We have leaned upon our Father throughout this journey, and tonight is one of those times where He is carrying us. My heart aches to see her in the condition she is in, and it is only through His strength and love and the prayers of all of you that we are able to continue, which we will surely do.

Day 2,004 PC
His Glory and Loving Embrace

January 10, 2018

Had I not had the privilege of being an active participant in Mildred's journey and had someone shared with me the details of her journey, I would have said, "You are lying" or "You must be writing a work of fiction." Few could have experienced the things Mildred experienced and live to tell about them more than 2,000 days later. Just think about that for a moment. It has been 2,004 days since we first began this journey on July 17, 2012. Yes, we have experienced many difficult and near life-ending times, and yet here we are still marching. The darker and more difficult the individual experience, the more glory and love God has displayed by taking us out of the valley and onto the highest mountaintop. This morning was just another shining example.

Mildred has had a difficult few weeks. Her cancer has spread. She has experienced a high level of pain in both of her sides where the cancer has invaded her ribs. She has holes in the tissues of her lungs, allowing air to escape into her chest cavity and forcing her heart to work harder. The projected end result of these issues is living on oxygen 24/7, taking daily pain medications, and involving hospice at some point. The only problem with this projected result is that the doctors forgot to check in with the Great Physician who has a different data interpretation and result in mind.

This past weekend, Mildred had severe fatigue, sleeping 14 consecutive hours from Sunday evening to Monday morning. However, on Monday, she began to have less pain, more awareness, and a better appetite. She continued to improve yesterday, not going to bed until almost midnight. This morning when she awoke and began to prepare for our meeting with her oncologist, she seemed more normal than she had been in a long time. She did not feel that she needed the oxygen and did not feel winded in any way. She ate breakfast before we left the house. She just seemed like the Mildred of two or three years ago in the earlier stages of our journey.

When we met with Dr. Lee, once again the medical results defied explanation. All her lab work is within normal ranges. Her CEA has declined to 328—a 40 percent decrease compared to 525 on November 6th. She is not experiencing any pain in either of her sides. Her pain has decreased significantly compared to Christmas morning and her hospital admission. Dr. Lee also said that based on her breathing this morning, she can use the oxygen on an as-needed basis instead of 24/7. He suggested the same for her pain meds. She is also receiving her next chemo treatment.

If I had not experienced firsthand what she went through Christmas morning, I would never know that she had suffered so much by looking at her today. The same holds true for this entire journey. A work of fiction? Not for a moment. It is simply God's glory and loving embrace displayed for all to see. I have said and will continue to say to anyone who asks me what they can do for us—just pray. The power of prayer is immeasurable and addresses all our needs. When your voices are lifting us up to our Father, we are strengthened. We are healed. Most importantly, we are *loved*.

Day 2,025 PC

We Keep Marching

January 31, 2018

Mildred has had some level of recurring fatigue over the past three weeks since her last chemo treatment, but all in all, she has had a good three weeks. We were able to host our life group for the first time since before Christmas. We hosted the salon's Christmas party this past Sunday. Mildred was able to visit the salon for the first time since before the holidays. Most of all, she was able to make enough of her beloved white chocolate peanut candy that she makes every holiday season so she could give some to the staff at the oncology clinic, particularly Dr. Lee and his wife, each employee at the salon, and several friends.

This past Friday she had a pulmonary stress test done at Princess Anne Hospital, and it did show that she will need to use oxygen when she is out and about as well as at night when she is sleeping. She will not need to use it as long as she is at home and relatively resting. We also met with Dr. Lee today to review her progress over these last three weeks. All of her labs have remained in normal ranges, and her CEA went from 328 to 326. It was not a significant decrease but certainly the continuation of a positive trend. The most positive number was her weight, which has increased from the upper 70-pound range to 92 pounds today. *Keep that cornbread coming!* She has not weighed more than 90 pounds since before the holidays, and she continues to have the luxury of eating anytime and almost anything she wants.

As we have throughout this journey, Mildred is ministering to others when she is able. Every time she is in the treatment room, it is like old home week. All the staff and a significant number of patients receive inspiration and blessings from her and share the pieces of their journey. She still remains in contact with certain family members of the patients who have departed, such as Maureen, the mother of Sherri, who most of you may remember from over three years ago. Maureen lives in California but will be here in Virginia next week and plans to visit Mildred. Mildred's story and her ability to share her faith and experiences continues to spread throughout the globe. She has said all along that until God tells her it is time to come home, she will continue to minister to whoever He puts in her path. The fields are still ripe for harvest, and we continue to work them to His glory.

Day 2,035 PC
Back in the Valley

February 10, 2018

Over the course of this past week, Mildred's health began to deteriorate. Aside from the fatigue she experienced as part of the normal chemo side effects, she began to develop a cough and congestion. As the week progressed, we saw her primary care physician, Dr. Javier, on Wednesday. After examining her and taking X-rays, he concluded that she had congestion in her lungs, but it had not progressed beyond that. Her flu test came back negative. He put her on antibiotics, which she immediately began taking. Over the next 48 hours, her cough and congestion continued to worsen, as well as her alertness and awakeness. As a result, we went to the ER at Princess Anne Hospital early Friday morning.

Talk about an overflow crowd, I have never in the 5+ years we have been there seen as many patients as were there on Friday. Even patients coming in on ambulance gurneys were lined up waiting to be seen. Mildred finally had the usual blood labs and CT scan. The conclusion was that she had developed pneumonia. They admitted her to the hospital and began administering IV antibiotics, pain medicine, and fluids. Shortly after her admission, her pulmonary doctor examined her, reviewed the CT scan, and then met with us. He described her pneumonia as extremely significant, the worst since he began treating her two years ago. He said they will continue to attack it with antibiotics but then discussed to what extent we wanted them to use life-saving measures in the form of a respirator or intubation. Mildred had all her wishes transcribed into an advanced care directive earlier on our journey, and she reiterated to him that she did not want to be kept alive by machines. His feeling was that with only antibiotics and other normal treatment measures, she would not survive. He had her transferred to the Intensive Care Unit where she was able to get some sleep. I began texting and calling family and friends to let them know of her condition and suggested that if they wanted to say goodbye, now was the time. I also mobilized our army of prayer warriors and asked them to begin praying.

I understand the gravity of what the pulmonary doctor said, but I also know that where Mildred is concerned, our Father has performed miracles before and is quite capable of performing them again. As we mobilize in prayer once more, I am asking everyone to please pray. Pray that God will not let her suffer and will bring forth healing in whatever manner He chooses. If once more He removes the infection from her body, we will stand on the mountaintop and shout His glorious name. If He chooses to bring her home, we will stand on the mountaintop and shout His glorious name. We have rested in His embrace since this journey began and will continue to do so now, no matter the outcome. We know there is no losing side on this journey. We are His, and He is ours. So do not let sadness and grief overcome you. Instead, lift up Mildred's name to Him, and pray as fervently and continuously as you have before. *We will continue to march!*

Day 2,036 PC
You Just Can't Make This Stuff Up

February 11, 2018

Last night Mildred's pulmonary doctor told us that the pneumonia Mildred has is so severe that even treating it with antibiotics will not overcome it. He was transferring her to the ICU where she could either be kept alive by machines or not come out alive. I immediately began mobilizing our army of prayer warriors, and over the next few hours, they prayed.

I left the hospital around 3:30 a.m. on Saturday morning to go home, shower, and change. I returned to the hospital around 6:00 a.m. When I returned, I noticed that her breathing did not seem as labored as it was. She awoke around 8:00 a.m. and was more alert and awake than she had been in the last 48 hours.

Around 9:00 a.m., she ate a small breakfast. Later in the morning, one of her pulmonary doctors' partners who had the weekend hospital duty came in to see her. He did a physical examination, spoke with her nurse, asked Mildred and me questions about her pain and her breathing. His conclusion was that she had made sufficient progress to be transferred out of ICU and into the Stepdown Unit. During the afternoon she was able to get out of the bed on her own power and spend approximately 15 minutes walking around the room with the use of a walker and the guidance of the physical therapist. I left the hospital around 7:00 p.m., and she was just going to sleep for the evening.

I do not have the right words to do justice to our Father's love for us and His response to the army of prayers. It simply is no coincidence that a multitude of voices were raised in prayer for her and within hours she began to show definite healing after the doctor said she would not live. How many times has God demonstrated His love for us on this journey, and how many more times will He? He will do it many more times than we will ever deserve. His love for us is infinite. His grace is limitless. His power is beyond words.

If He took Mildred or me home tonight, we would still have so much to be thankful for. Please continue to share her story with all you know, and let it inspire others as He has inspired us. Thanks so much to each of you for raising us up in prayer, and may His blessings fall on you as they have on us. Please continue to pray for us so she may come home soon and resume her service to Him.

Day 2,039 PC

Climbing the Final Mountain

February 14, 2018

My heart is breaking as I write this. The progress Mildred displayed between Friday and Sunday equals how fast she has deteriorated since then. While she did move to the Stepdown Unit in the hospital, she is now on her final climb to the mountaintop. They are continuing to pump her full of antibiotics and pain medicine, but the pneumonia, combined with the expanding cancer, has made her breathing very difficult. Over the last 60 hours, she has gone from breathing through an oxygen line at a 2-liter level to a 6-liter level and is now breathing with an Opti-Flow machine. Unlike a respirator, which her advanced care directive prohibits, this machine pushes oxygen into her lungs so they can function.

A respirator is a machine that actually breathes for you. Even with the Opti-Flow machine, her body is wracking with every breath. In addition, she has begun experiencing periods of delirium where she is talking to people who are not in the room and some who died years ago. She is answering questions with totally unrelated subjects.

While a miracle is still possible, according to the medical staff, she has deteriorated where she can no longer be sent home because her condition requires 24/7 attention. They expect her to live a matter of days, not weeks.

When Mildred decides, which I expect will be imminent, they will place her on in-hospital hospice. That means they will stop treating her with medicine other than pain medicine and try to make her as comfortable as possible. She will be assisted in her breathing as she currently is until she either says to take the oxygen away or takes her last breath.

While the grief of watching her in such pain and then losing her is already upon me, I take solace in that I have *no doubt* where she is headed and that she will be free of any pain. We promised in our wedding vows to love and cherish each other always and forever, and that is what we will continue to do. I have prayed to our Father that when the time comes to please take her home quickly and do not let her suffer. He has heard my prayers and answered them, and for that I am extremely grateful. Please continue to pray that He will give me the strength to navigate these last few days before we have the celebration to end all celebrations as we give praise for Mildred, the life she has led, and who she is. Thank you so much for what each of you have done on this journey.

Day 2,040 PC

The Gates of Glory

February 15, 2018

Mildred passed through the Gates of Glory at 7:50 a.m. this morning. The Lord heard my prayers and did not let her suffer. From Sunday evening until this morning, her condition rapidly deteriorated. Yesterday morning the doctor told me she had days, not weeks to live. But our Father did not let it go even that long. I spent the night with her, and she continued to become more and more delirious. The medical staff increased her pain meds, and although she had difficulty breathing until the end, her level of discomfort had declined. She had a few lucid moments during the last hours of her life, and we were able one last time to say how much we loved each other.

She truly was my special angel that the Lord blessed me with for almost 40 years. I certainly did not deserve someone as special as she was, but I think our Father determined that I needed all the help I could get, and she was the person up to the job. I will love her *forever and always*.

I am in the process of finalizing the funeral service details, and as soon as I have everything, I will post it. We will truly have a celebration of her life just as she wanted—no tears of sadness, only tears of joy. She now resides with our Heavenly Father, and I look forward to when my time comes.

'Til we meet again, my love.

Day 2,040 PC

A Love Story

February 15, 2018

It has been 13 hours since Mildred was called home. As I sit here this evening and reflect on our life, I am reminded of the 1970 Oscar-winning movie *Love Story*. That is what I was privileged to live, including its ending. Mildred and I came from such different backgrounds and locations. I was a poor white kid who grew up in a South Philly rowhouse, and she was an American Indian farmgirl who grew up in North Carolina. We were blessed to meet and fall in love.

While we had our ups and downs like any marriage, we were always there for each other. After the first 10 years, we truly found our place with each other and lived a life full of passion, compassion, and purpose. Did we have to learn to compromise or allow the other person to have it their way? Absolutely. But during that time, our lives became so intertwined that we were like one. She was truly my heart and soul, and tonight there is a broken heart within me.

During these last five and a half years as we progressed on our cancer journey, many people said how strong I must be to do for her as I was blessed to do. While our Father gave me strength, it paled in comparison to the strength He gave her to handle the physical, emotional, and mental strains of the cancer. She was definitely the one with strength. My love for her was what drove me to do what I did, and I would gladly do it again. She often said, "He is my rock," but she was my rock long before I was ever hers. She made me who I am today.

Even now, I feel like she is just at the hospital getting well so we can resume our journey. I know this is no longer the case, but she will be part of my life every day as I go forward. I will love her *always and forever* as we promised in our wedding vows. She will be with me every day as I continue to feel her presence in our house. As I prepare to enter a new phase of my life, and most likely the last phase, I believe whatever my purpose will be in the future will be a direct result of the last 40 years and the angel I was blessed to share my life with.

Rest easy, my darling. I will see you soon.

GAY, RN, OCN (ONCOLOGY NURSE)

Mildred was a gift and a blessing to all who knew her. Meeting Mildred was certainly my pleasure, although it was under the most unpleasant of circumstances. She had Stage 4 cancer, and I was her nurse. Arriving to the treatment room with her clothing, makeup, and hair impeccably done and Bob at her side, Mildred smiled, and her spirit lifted the heavy hearts of those in her presence. Camaraderie ensued from hours of sharing and caring together while receiving biweekly intravenous chemotherapy treatments.

Mildred rose daily with renewed spiritual strength and determination even though her body was becoming more and more fragile. The years of cancer along with the side effects of chemotherapy were taking its toll on her physically. She and Bob never seemed to lose their sense of peace throughout this difficult journey. The cancer progressed, as did her treatments. Mildred continued to march on as her health was slowly deteriorating from this unyielding invasion. The duration of her journey is a testament to her unwavering faith and her willingness to serve and trust in the Lord. Mildred's peace and calmness throughout her care worried me at times. It was as if she were in denial. Instead, this proved to be acceptance—acceptance of the Lord's plan. I will forever hold my memories of Mildred and Bob close to my heart.

EPILOGUE

For the first four months after Mildred was called home, the pain of loss and grief was an everyday, all-day occurrence. I felt like I was continually being punched in the stomach, and my heart ached so much. Mildred and I spent 40 years together, and she was such an integral part of my life. The thing I miss the most was the end of each day when we cuddled in bed. I used to tell her that it was the best part of my day. That void has been tremendous. One evening in early June, I went to bed feeling this way. When I woke up the next morning, I felt as if Mildred and our Heavenly Father had laid their hands on me and infused me with the Holy Spirit. I no longer had the overwhelming pain of loss and grief. Instead, I felt like I could run a marathon. Since that morning, I have been full of joy and energy. I never recall feeling this way at any other time in my life. I have received so many blessings, far beyond anything I ever deserved.

After that morning, I knew what I was called to do—minister! At first, I thought continuing to operate the salon was part of my ministry. We would completely remodel and grow it so it could provide funding and opportunities for ministry activities. However, the estimated cost to do that was approximately $150,000. While I could obtain the financing to do that, the landlord would only agree to a 10-year lease as opposed to a five-year lease with an additional five-year option. That would mean I would be 76 before the lease was up. It was a time when I felt like God was telling me one thing, but by listening and praying, it became apparent that He was telling me not to do that.

In February 2020, I financed the sale and sold the salon to two of Mildred's long-time employees who now own and operate it. After the sale, I continued ministering to members of New Life Church who were going through their own journeys, be it cancer or other terminal illnesses. I began working with two nonprofit cancer patient organizations that provide meals, transportation, and financial grants to patients. I minister to individuals who have lost their spouse to cancer or something else. I provide one-on-one counseling to whoever our Father brings across my path. As a result of these efforts and having completed various educational courses, on April 1, 2021, I officially became a licensed chaplain of New Life Church.

As of today, July 13, 2024, I continue to perform these duties and serve. However, there is one thing I have not yet completed. From the first day of our journey and as it progressed, Mildred and I had written the components of our story—from childhood through her homecoming. However, when she was called home, I put down the manuscript. While I said I would finish the book and publish it, I could not bring myself to do so. I was able to minister to people with cancer and other conditions, but finishing and publishing the book meant reading and reliving every single day of our journey and all the details. I put our work on the book away in my office files, and for the next six years, I focused on the rest of my ministry. Then, in what I call God's lightning bolt to me, I went searching in my office for the files the week of July 8, 2024. When I found them,

EPILOGUE

I began putting all the pieces together to complete the first draft of the book. In fact, as I write this Epilogue, it is July 13, 2024. It was 44 years ago on this very date that Mildred and I exchanged wedding vows. I have begun researching Christian publishers with whom I can partner to publish and distribute the story. Whether I speak with one person at a time or a thousand people at a time, I will spend the last phase of my life uplifting, inspiring, and sharing what our Father has done for Mildred and me and how we have been so blessed throughout our lives. Neither Mildred nor I could have navigated our cancer journey without the love and support of our Heavenly Father and a broad network of friends and family we have been blessed with.

As I look back over my soon-to-be 70 years of life and my 40 years of sharing my life with Mildred, as well as the 69 years she was blessed to live, it is totally and completely apparent to me that our Heavenly Father had a definite plan for the two of us. So many things happened in each of our lives that cannot be explained, except to say, "it was a God-thing." I know our story was meant to be shared with others so they, too, can be inspired to love our Father just as He loves us. No matter what anyone is facing in life, no matter how deep or wide the valley is that anyone is confronted with, they can know that God is there walking right beside them. In the hardest times—medical, financial, marital, or family relationships—He will pick you up and carry you through if you simply believe and reach out to Him.

Mildred and I knew from the very first day of our cancer journey—and I still know it to this day—that our Father continues to say:

I've got this!

www.ingramcontent.com/pod-product-compliance
Lightning Source LLC
Chambersburg PA
CBHW071736150426
43191CB00010B/1596